Naughty But
Nice

Anita Naik is a freelance writer and journalist who writes regularly for a variety of UK magazines including *Now, First, New Woman, Eve* and *Red*. Specialising in health, sex and lifestyle issues, Anita was also the sex columnist on *Just 17* and *More,* and advice columnist on *Closer* magazine.

Anita is also the author of:
Babe Bible
Pocket Babe
The Lazy Girl's Guide to Beauty
The Lazy Girl's Guide to Good Health
The Lazy Girl's Guide to Good Sex
The Lazy Girl's Guide to a Fabulous Body
The Lazy Girl's Party Guide
The Lazy Girl's Guide to Men
The New You

Naughty But Nice

THE NO-EXCUSES GUIDE TO GETTING WHAT YOU WANT

ANITA NAIK

PIATKUS

℘℘ *Visit the Piatkus website!*

Piatkus publishes a wide range of best-selling fiction and non-fiction, including books on health, mind, body & spirit, sex, self-help, cookery, biography and the paranormal.

If you want to:
- read descriptions of our popular titles
- buy our books over the Internet
- take advantage of our special offers
- enter our monthly competition
- learn more about your favourite Piatkus authors

VISIT OUR WEBSITE AT: www.piatkus.co.uk

Copyright © 2006 by Anita Naik
www.anitanaik.co.uk

First published in 2006 by
Piatkus Books Ltd
5 Windmill Street
London W1T 2JA

e-mail: info@piatkus.co.uk

The moral right of the author has been asserted

A catalogue record for this book is available from the British Library

ISBN 0 7499 2694 5

Text design and setting by Goldust Design
Edited by Jan Cutler
Illustrations by Robyn Neild

This book has been printed on paper manufactured with respect for the environment using wood from managed sustainable resources

Data manipulation by Phoenix Photosetting, Chatham, Kent
www.phoenixphotosetting.co.uk

Printed and bound in Great Britain by
Mackays of Chatham, Chatham, Kent

Contents

Acknowledgements

Thanks to Alice Davis for celebrity gossip, Vegas tips and being really good fun to work with, and all the naughty-but-nice girls who filled out the questionnaires for this book, shared their secrets with me and made me laugh with their replies; especially, Kate Grainger, Fiona Robertson, Franca Tranza, Anita Flowers and Jenni Baxter.

Introduction

Do you need a self-esteem make-over? If you feel your life lacks adventure, your looks are missing that certain je ne sais quoi and your attitude's about as bold as a small fluffy kitten, then it's likely you need to boost your self-worth and give in to what's known as a naughty-but-nice attitude. Naughty, as in living and going for what you want, and nice, as in finally getting what you want, for a change!

According to a report published by the mental healthcare providers, The Priory Group (March 2006), millions of us currently suffer from 'Not-Good-Enough' syndrome and have self-esteem that's so low that it adversely affects our relationships, work prospects, body image and quality of life. According to the research results, 57 per cent of us are people-pleasers, eager to put our own needs on hold for others. Fifty per cent know they are their own worst critics and routinely let a little voice inside them stop them from reaching their goal. A mammoth 39 per cent of us don't say what we think because we are worried about what others might say, and 36 per cent of us say that how we feel about ourselves depends on how other people treat us. On top of all of this, nearly a quarter of us say we're perfectionists with unrealistic expectations of life, including personal relationships and career development.

It sounds depressing but it isn't, because acknowledging you have low self-esteem is a great starting point: it's only when you realise that you are suffering from a negative self-image that you start wanting to change and actually start changing your life. This needn't be a radically different life but a life that's definitely more exciting and broader than it currently is. A life that's bold and a life where, when you look in the mirror, an involuntary groan doesn't escape your lips. So if you're feeling a bit 'bland and blah' about yourself, and hate what you've become (or are turning into) then you've come to the right place, because *Naughty But Nice* can show you how to chase your dreams, change your attitude, find your inner sexiness and have the added oomph of true diva-style!

Better still, unlike other makeover, reinvention and change-my-life books, this book is not just about what you're doing wrong, but about what you're not doing at all. So if you have reached a point in your life where you want to scream because life seems to be hurtling past you and where each birthday fills you with dread and your list of things not yet done grows longer than the list of things you have done, it's finally time to become the person you are inside. The person who dreams big (or used to), the person who has the guts to grab what she wants, and finds the gusto to throw herself into things even when she's scared.

Discover, too, how to feel better about your body, improve your self-image, find an attitude and not give up on the things you want to do because you feel too old, too stuck or too tired. And before you say it – yes, you can do it, because living a naughtier life is not about having more time, more money and more energy, it's simply about learning how to say yes to life. That's yes to scary new challenges, yes to crazy ventures and yes to suggestions you previously turned up your nose at out of fear. All you have to do is take a deep breath, dive in and find out how to start making things happen for yourself.

How do I know it works? Well, after years of being a self-confessed good girl who was too scared to say what she wanted, and to swim with her head under the water, never mind drive through heavy traffic or join a gym, in case someone saw how my thighs met in the middle, I woke up and realised I was tired of thinking: 'Is this as good as it gets?'. So I started saying yes and I let go of worrying about what others thought of me (hard but not impossible).

In the process I ended up doing some very 'not me' things such as: having a radical makeover – something I'd previously thought was too vain and too bimbo-ish. I dumped needy friends who got me down (the guilt wasn't that bad), and even went on prime-time television to promote a book (previously I'd always been too scared). On the adventure front I tried abseiling down a cliff face (horrible), learned to Thai box (I have the bruises to prove it) and started speaking up for myself.

By jumping in the naughty end of the pool I learned that while good girls do have some fun, naughty girls have more, and even though you do sometimes sink and fall flat on your face, mostly you get to float, because a naughtier attitude takes you further than months of planning, years of saving and hours spent at the gym. What's more, having fun and doing stuff that scares the hell out of you is a huge learning curve that opens up your life and gives you a fast track to fulfilling dreams that you thought you'd packed away years ago. It boosts your confidence, gives you that devil-may-care attitude and encourages you to take risks in all areas of your life.

So, if you want to revamp your attitude, find your sexy side and focus on being desire-driven for a change, you've come to the right place. Follow the exercises throughout this book and you'll find out how to trust your instincts, take control, get noticed and have a blast. Go on, give it a try – isn't it time to have some more fun in your life?

Desire

Introduction

What do you desire in your life? Aside from bigger/smaller boobs, winning the lottery and a movie-star husband? When was the last time you sat down and thought carefully about your secret desires, wants and needs? And I'm not talking domestic needs or career wants, but simple, honest desires for YOU! If the answer is years ago, it's worth remembering that knowing what you want and need is the key to living a happy and fulfilled life. Why? Well, because it's the fulfilment of what you desire that determines how happy you feel and how happy you are in your own skin, or, as the experts say, how authentically you end up living your life.

Quash your needs, ignore what you desire or just simply forget about what you want out of life because you're too busy getting things done, then the chances are you're going to be someone who wakes up one day and feels unhappy, depressed and plain fed up. If that sounds familiar, you're not alone; most of us have spent a lifetime trying to please someone else and be what we're not, which is why it's time to give yourself a wake-up talk and consider just what you want and why. Maybe you think you're too old, or too poor to go for it. Or perhaps you think it's just too late to go after want you want and make your dreams come true.

Maybe, you even believe you're just too busy making a living to bother about what you want. If so, it's worth knowing that it's never too late to be who you want to be in life.

Life is full of examples of late bloomers: women who took up writing at 70 and became world-renowned authors, actresses who suddenly won an Oscar at 60, or businesswomen who made their first million in their fifties. While I am not advocating waiting until you're grey to make your impact, the point is that if they can do it so can you. The good news is that success and a sense of fulfilment are not just for people in their early twenties – they are for anyone willing to get out there and grab life.

Reinvention is also on offer for all: look at all the women who lose half their body weight after a lifetime of being fat, or those who decide they are going to run a marathon, climb a mountain or even start their own business after years of being bored out of their minds. Or even women who end up single after 20 years of marriage and blossom overnight into gorgeous beings who have lives twice as exciting as before. It's not an accident or fluke, it's all down to rediscovering who they are, deep down inside.

The fact is, you have one life, and if you currently hate where you are, you owe it to yourself to change things and cram it with as much fun, happiness and a sense of achievement as you can. What's more, it's not selfish to put your desires first even if you have kids or are part of a couple, but it is martyrdom if you decide to put your needs second and then make everyone else feel bad about what's happening to you. Which means that if you're fed up and can't remember the last time you let rip with a loud laugh, and/or have no idea when you last felt euphoric with joy, it's time to refocus and fight back.

'I'm a huge believer in having a consuming passion, because I think it's important to have one thing that you want to do and love to do that has nothing to do with your love life, or your job or your family. For me swimming is my escape, something that I do every day that's just for me and no one else. It's not about fitness, it's about being underwater and being quiet and peaceful and about having some me-time.' Charlotte, 26

Pinpointing your desires is where it all begins, and the strategy is simple: think about what you want and why, and not just in a serious way. Wanting more fun, less gravity and generally more adventure is what life is all about, alongside the day-to-day business of living, work, relationships and bills.

Quiz

WHAT DO YOU DESIRE?

Self-awareness is crucial when it comes to making
changes of any type. No matter how well you
think you know yourself and how you ended up
where you are, the chances are you're missing the bigger
picture. The following quiz and exercises are designed to give you a
clearer insight into your personality and desires. Go with your gut feeling
when answering.

1. **When people come to you with their problems you:**
a. Suggest they just get on with it. (B)
b. End up talking about your own problems. (A)
c. Cry with them. (C)
d. End up becoming embroiled in their problems. (D)

2. **How many of your childhood dreams have you fulfilled?**
a. None of them have worked out. (C)
b. You didn't have any. (D)
c. Fewer than three, but you're still trying. (A)
d. The ones that everyone else achieved. (B)

3. **When you lose out on a promotion or a good work experience you:**
a. Aren't surprised because you're not lucky. (D)
b. Suspect you weren't good enough. (B)

c. Believe something better is about to happen. (A)

d. Blame someone else. (C)

4. Family and friends consider you:

a. An easygoing and funny person. (A)

b. Someone to be relied upon. (B)

c. Stable and honest. (C)

d. A bit of a loser. (D)

5. Winning the lottery would make your dreams come true because:

a. You would invest wisely and live off the income. (B)

b. You would never have to do anything again. (D)

c. You could do anything you wanted. (A)

d. It would make people take you seriously. (C)

6. When you spend time with women who are more successful than you you feel:

a. Despondent. (C)

b. Competitive. (B)

c. Small. (D)

d. Equal to them. (A)

7. When you think of yourself in five years' time, you see yourself:

a. Older. (B)

b. Hopefully thinner. (C)

c. Sadder. (D)

d. More successful. (A)

8. **At dinner you are seated next to a famous soap actress.**
   How do you feel?
a. Unworthy. (D)
b. Happy you've got a chance to impress. (A)
c. Worried about what to say. (B)
d. Eager to impress them. (C)

9. **Your best friend asks you to make a speech at her wedding. You:**
a. Jump at the chance. (A)
b. Say yes, but panic from this point on. (B)
c. Say no because you hate putting yourself in the limelight. (D)
d. Say no because you know you'll get it wrong. (C)

10. **Your friends catch you and your partner having a fight. You:**
a. Pretend nothing is going on. (A)
b. Tell them exactly what you're rowing about. (C)
c. Put the argument on hold. (B)
d. Reassure them that it was all your fault. (D)

Results

Add up all the answers you gave that were followed by (A) and then those followed by (B), and so on. Then see which score was the highest. If you scored highest on the (A) answers that makes you a Big Dreamer, see below. If you scored highest on the (B) answers that makes you Ms Practical, and so on.

BIG DREAMER (mostly As)

You know your desires, needs and wants, in fact you know them so well that you enjoy spending more time dreaming about them than making practical steps to get there. Why spoil the dream with reality? Because in your heart of hearts you don't really believe you can make it big, so you dream big instead and live in 'I'd do it if ...' land, meaning: 'I'd do it if I had more money, more time, more help', and so on. The good news is that big dreamers do make it big once they start to believe in themselves.

As someone who does her best to fit in and meet other people's expectations you are very popular, and with your big dreams you have clearer goals than you think. And you know what would make you happy. Your aim should be to move beyond daydreaming and bring your desires into the real world with a plan of action. Remember: sink or swim, failure is always better than wishing you could turn back the clock and have your time again.

MS PRACTICAL (mostly Bs)

You know what you want and why, but you shut yourself down with a million 'yes, buts' in order to avoid disappointment and failure. Practical and savvy by nature, the good news is that everyone believes in you except yourself. Meaning, you are the smart girl who doesn't know that she's smart and you are just the kind of person to fulfil your desires if only you didn't put up hurdles in front of what you want.

Being too busy/too tired/too old are not real excuses – if you wanted to write a novel you would find the time, if you wanted to get fit you could, and if you wanted to have a more exciting life you know how to find it. To combat your mindset, put your practicality to better use and remind yourself that you are gifted with the ability to see things through; when faced with a hurdle, think your way over, round or under it, and you'll get to where you want to be.

DISTRACTED DREAMER (mostly Cs)

Distracted – you? How many times have you done this quiz and not read these answers? The fact is you have a short attention span and are easily distracted, and you are happier to take short cuts and/or accept what seems like the inevitable than turn round and go for what you want. Why? Because you feel comfortable where you are, and, even though now and again you feel despondent, on the whole you think: 'Why rock the boat?' The only problem is that if you're honest you do feel as if you're living a half-life – one where something is missing. The missing part is the excitement of going after what you want, taking risks and fulfilling your desires. To move off your square of security you have to shake up your life, focus on what you want and why, and then seek out a little bit of discomfort to get to where you want to be.

SLOW STARTER (mostly Ds)

You find it very difficult to be yourself in the way you'd like to be because while you have a vague idea of what would make you more confident you don't know how to get there, so you give up before trying. This means you're happy to let others decide who you are and what you want, and adaptable enough to let their predictions become truths. The trouble is at times you probably feel despondent and defeated by life, and entertain the thought of change without knowing where to start.

What you need to realise is that you don't always have to sacrifice your own desires to make people like and love you. Be who you want to be, even if that goes against the grain, because it's this that will help you to go after your dreams and start making them come true.

Desire
FACING THE FACTS

If you were to make a critique of your life so far, what grade would you give yourself for reaching your goals? A 'B' for good try, a 'C' for could do better or a 'D' for dismal effort? If you fall into the 'I've never reached a single goal' category, the good news is that you're not alone and don't need a slap on the wrist or intensive therapy to 'get better', but you do need a lesson in boosting your self-worth.

So here's a quick crash course in self-esteem, or rather, what happens when you have a lack of it. Firstly, if you think you don't have a problem with self-esteem, think back to when you were 15 years old and in one of those endless conversations with yourself about how to be prettier, thinner, sexier and cleverer. Now, when was the last time you had a conversation with yourself about those things? Was it (a) last week; (b) last night; (c) in the last five minutes; or (d) when you were 15?

Aside from option (d), if you fell into any of the other categories, it's time to admit that you have flagging self-esteem. It may not be killing you but I'll bet it has affected your choice of career, your choice of relationships and your decisions about fulfilling your dreams.

As an ex-low-self-esteemer I know how it feels to play it safe in every area of life, as do most of the women I interviewed for this book, and most of the women who write in to me at my advice column. I've spoken to women who have stayed with men they knew were not right for them because it was better than being single and alone. I know attractive women who dress down, wearing dark colours so that they can escape into the shadows and hide their less-than-perfect bits, and, personally, I've tried hard to please other people so that they would like me no matter what.

'I think innate confidence to go after what you want in life stems from being faced with challenges in life through which you know you can navigate and survive. Physically, self-esteem stems from feeling happy about your body, but if your body is not how you want it to be, it helps if you still see yourself as an intelligent, valuable human being in your interactions with others. I also have a job, friends and a life outside of all that which gives me a sense of fulfilment and self-worth and makes me realise that it's never too late to go after what you want.'
Kate, 28

While playing it safe has its benefits – that is, you always feel safe – it's also an ideal way to quash your desires and ensure that you don't get what you want out of life. So, if you're tired of hiding in a corner and moaning about what hasn't happened, here's how to start transforming your life.

STEP ONE

WARNING – desire-free zone ahead!

Everything significant starts with a vision, a dream and a first step, the problem is that many of us are miserable and spend so much time thinking about why we are unhappy that we forget to think about what we actually want out of life. Which is why step one is about positive thinking and a spot of daydreaming! Instead of zoning out to your iPod or losing yourself in a domestic chore every time you have 20 minutes to yourself, just stop and think about your life in the positive. Grab a notebook and write down:

1. What do you want?
2. What would make you happy?
3. What desires are, as yet, unfulfilled?

And remember: when thinking about your new vision, think positively and don't allow yourself to slip in all those negative reasons why you can't do something. If you're not a positive thinker this bit can be hard. Personally, I believe in positive thinking, simply because I spent years indulging in negative thinking and saw how well that worked for me. You know the scenario, you wake up feeling blue, spill your coffee all over you, fall down the stairs and think this is the worst day ever and then proceed to make it the worst day ever! Thankfully it works the other way, too, which means you'll only ever be as happy as your expectations allow you to be. So, if you want a wild and naughty life but continually think, 'I'm so boring and dull, no wonder no one likes me' that's kind of the life you're going to get.

Negative mental tactics that stop us from having the life we want are:

- **All-or-nothing thinking: the belief that things that are going wrong is a sign that there's no point in trying. As they say, a mistake is a mistake only if you don't learn anything from it.**
- **A 'should' list: these are commands we give ourselves about how we think we have to live our life, such as I should eat healthily, I should work harder. They don't work because they are not necessarily our real wants.**
- **Magnification: where you magnify your faults and flaws and all the things that could go wrong, and minimise your skills.**
- **The 'I'm being realistic' retort: your reply when anyone tries to get you to look at the upside of life. You assume yours is a more authentic view of life.**
- **Thinking you have bad odds stacked against you: this is a belief that things are different for you, that somehow you're unlucky, and although it worked for 99 out of 100 people you're guaranteed to be the one person it doesn't work for.**

To shake yourself out of this state (and you can) the trick is to do something completely out of character whenever you feel negative thinking sinking into your brain, such as jump up and down on the spot, sing loudly in your head or even hold an ice cube in your hand (extreme, but it will instantly stop negative thinking). Friends who do this say the following techniques also do the trick: recalling a funny incident, listening to loud rock music, throwing cold water on their face, going for a breath of fresh air, dancing madly around the room, or even knocking back a shot of whisky (although an espresso is probably more work friendly).

On a long-term basis, changing your state can have staggering implications on how you feel about yourself and how you live your life, and you'll be amazed at the difference: a new haircut, changing the colour or shape of your clothes (see Style for more on this), using a stronger voice and tone, having opinions (see Attitude), losing weight and taking up something new, will all have an effect on your life and the way you think.

Anna, 27, can vouch for the power of this because when she lost just 4.5kg (10lb) not only was she shocked every time she looked in the mirror but also friends who had known her for years suddenly started treating her in a very different way. It wasn't that she'd suddenly turned into a supermodel but that she'd gone from 'cuddly Anna' to sexy Anna. This was not just because she had dropped a clothes size but because she truly felt different about herself and so started to act differently, focus differently and change her life.

The aim of any personality breakout like Anna's is simply a way of taking a first step to the new and naughty you – so find something that gives you a positive reaction and makes you feel good, and you'll be amazed at how much confidence it gives you to keep on changing.

Whatever you think of, it's vital that you do it in a positive way, and ride through the initial discomfort. For example, take Claire, 30, who after years of wearing black, baggy clothes and feeling lost in the crowd bought a red dress and wore it to work. She had always wanted to be the centre of attention and feel attractive but she was shocked by the power of her statement, because she was literally the talk of her office all day. You might think, 'Great!', but it was a step too far in Claire's mind, because she spent all day feeling insulted by how much difference a colour could make, and about the attention she was receiving because of it. So she raced back to wearing her baggy clothes.

In contrast, take Zoe, who had always considered herself clumsy; she took secret salsa lessons for a whole year and then wowed her entire office at the Christmas party. The confidence her turn on the dance floor gave her did more than boost her persona at work – it also opened doors to a whole new life and a whole new lease of confidence that went beyond her dancing, simply because she realised she could really do anything she set her mind to.

CLUES YOU'VE HAD A DESIRE MELTDOWN ARE:

- Telling yourself it's okay always to put others first.
- No longer knowing what it is you want from life.
- Thinking you should be grateful and not want more.
- Not being able to say no to people you love.
- Feeling you can't express your hopes to anyone.
- Feeling ashamed that you want more than you have.
- Letting friends and family dismiss your dreams as silly.
- Feeling something is missing from your life.
- Not having faith in your own decisions and desires.
- Feeling immobilised with anxiety about the future.
- Feeling you are being left behind by your friends and peers.
- Thinking this is as good as it gets.
- Not expecting anything good, so you won't be disappointed.
- Feeling you have somehow missed the boat.

So, if you want to get out of a life that's low and spice it up, you need to start unravelling what has made you give up on your dreams. Start by trying the following exercise.

INSTANT NAUGHTY TASK
Call up, email or find a person who actually lives out one of your dreams and ask them for advice.

16

EXERCISE ONE

List three things you daydream about to make yourself feel better when you're blue.

1. ....
   ....
2. ....
   ....
3. ....
   ....

Now ask yourself:
1. Which elements of the above daydream (or which dreams) would you love to be a reality?
2. What could you do in the next hour to bring a dream closer to a reality?
3. What's stopping you from doing this (if it's a fundamental thing like your job, money or time, what could you do to change this)?

STEP TWO

Live for now

I once said to a friend that he should learn to live for the present and start living his life the way he wanted. He said, 'As if; I would just spend all my days getting drunk and watching TV!', which leads me to another important point: living for now doesn't means chucking your responsibilities out of the window and loafing about doing nothing. It means spending your days more effectively and living out your dreams, which means that unless you're 99 years old and on your deathbed you can change your life, problems and woes, and make your life more exciting, no matter where you are right now.

> 'I used to be someone who wanted to be famous, wanted to be rich and dreamt of having it all, but I'm stuck in a job I hate, bored and have no idea what happened to all my plans. I can't remember when I gave up.' Steph, 27

What's more, forget the excuses, you don't need money, you can find the time and you can have the life you want as long as you're determined to work at it. I meet plenty of people in my daily life who say to me, 'It's okay for you, I hate my job, I would love to spend my days writing books but I don't have the time/space/computer to do it on.' Well, if one of the world's most famous writers, Stephen King, could write his first novel on a notepad while holding down two jobs and bringing up his kids with his wife in a one-bedroomed apartment, I'm guessing anyone can. Easy for me to say but when you look at someone else's life (and I am as guilty of this as the next person) and feel envious of the ease with which they get to do things, the reality is you're not seeing all the graft and sacrifices that they made (and maybe even still make) to get there. The reason they keep going is because when you're going after something you want, the hard work is worth it and often doesn't even feel like graft and sacrifice.

This is why it's a choice to give up on your dreams, and whereas it might be a choice pushed along by outside factors like time and money, somewhere down the line you have to admit to yourself that you made a decision to give up on who you want to be. This may be due to disappointment, setbacks, fear or simply how you were taught to live, but all these things influence the way we think and act in the present.

The good news is that studies show self-esteem and positive beliefs are something you can learn, and doing so will increase your resilience, and improve your chances of a successful outcome in whatever you do. Of course, it's not easy to move from good girl to naughty girl overnight, so to discover how and why you got to where you are right now it's important to look back to where you came from. For most of us this means going back to our childhoods and working out clues that will show us why we behave the way we do.

For example, do you have strong memories of how your parents lived and spoke about their dreams? Maybe you remember your parents at odds with each other about what they wanted to do in their lives. Or do you remember them always putting off what they really wanted for another day, or did they live a wild and lavish lifestyle or tell you that it didn't

EXERCISE TWO

To help yourself look at the past, ask yourself:
1. What positive and negative messages were you given about following your dreams when growing up?
2. When you did something wild/crazy/adventurous, how did your parents respond to your actions?
3. Did your parents have differing views from each other on how to live life?
4. What regrets did your parents have about their lives?

matter how hard you tried because you're either lucky or you're not? These messages are important because they lay the foundations of how you now think about life. Your attitude towards how you live today will be either a replica of your parents or a rebellion against their attitude. Whether you like it or not, the way our parents lived their lives affects how we live life now. For example, are you like Jenny, 38, who lives for today after growing up with parents who lived a frugal life so that they could 'live for tomorrow'? Or are you like Frances, 28, who, like her mother, feels 'There is no point in trying as I am not the sort of person to get anywhere'? Or maybe you are like Kara, 32, who is afraid to 'reach for the stars in case I am disappointed, like my mum always was'.

Knowing what your past life lessons were is a huge part in changing your beliefs about your ability to go after what you want. Try the following exercise to highlight your thought process further.

EXERCISE THREE

1. Does your current lifestyle and behaviour reflect your mother's style, your father's style or neither?
2. List two beliefs you hold about women who are sexy and successful?

a. ....

b. ....

3. List two beliefs you hold about why you haven't fulfilled your desires?

a. ....

b. ....

The good news is that beliefs are not written in stone, which means you can change the ones you've listed above at any time with a simple decision to try a different route. A simple way to do this is to list all three desires (old or new) in one column and then next to them write why you believe they haven't come true.

For example, here is the list for Helen, 30, who is single:

Desire	Why it hasn't happened
1. To get married	No decent men out there
2. Go travelling	I'll be lonely if I go alone and it's dangerous
3. To open my own card design company	I'm no good at business

When you have your list, go back over it and question your beliefs about why they haven't happened. Pretend you're interviewing someone you don't know, and play devil's advocate and ask challenging questions.

In Helen's case, is it really true that there are no decent men?

- **What does she mean by decent?**
- **What could she do to meet more men?**

Regarding travelling:

- **How could she safeguard herself and still go?**
- **Could she find a travelling partner or could she go as part of a tour?**

Regarding opening her own business:

- **Where could she seek help to open a business?**
- **What areas does she feel weak in?**

> **INSTANT NAUGHTY TASK**
> **Do something today that you have always wanted to do but never had the guts to try — smile at a guy you fancy, skip work, have an impromptu dinner party and invite your neighbours.**

STEP THREE

Think about what you want

Do you think you know what you want and how to get it? If so, how come it isn't making you happy? The reality is that most of us have convinced ourselves that we know what would make us happy and in most cases this list probably consists of:

- New clothes
- A thinner body
- A boyfriend/new boyfriend
- More money
- A better job
- Marriage and kids
- Bigger/smaller breasts
- An ageproof skin

However, these are not desires, these are wants that we've learned give us instant gratification, or desires that other people have foisted upon us, or give us needs that society tells us we should want. That's not to say you've been duped or have been brainwashed into wanting these things, it's just that if none of the above feels enough right now, somewhere deep inside you is a desire that you're quashing. If you're stuck for where to start, think back to the last time your hands went sweaty with excitement or your heart pounded with happiness. Can you recall why this happened? Can you remember how it made you feel? And what do you want to do right now that gives you the same sensation?

If you're completely stuck, one good way to find out what you want is to open yourself up to a variety of new things that you've never considered before. For example, if you're bored with being on the treadmill of get-up-go-to-work-have-lunch-work-some-more-come-home-watch-TV-go-to-bed-and-start-again, broaden your life and find for yourself what's known as a consuming passion. Forget what you're good at and what you're not, and experiment, because the secret to finding a naughty passion is literally to cram your life with things – things you love, new things, weird things and challenging things. Different books, films, hobbies, sports, creative tasks, practical skills – the list is endless, and it's all there for you to sample.

Consuming passions I've spotted in other people range from diving every weekend (not anywhere exotic, usually the local pool with a local diving club) to graphic novels, horses, cooking and even BMX riding (and she's 26, by the way). To find your own consuming passion, think back to when you were a kid and what you liked to do the most. Were you an outside-of-the-house kind of kid who liked to ride her bike or skateboard, or someone who liked to read or draw or make things? The clues to your consuming passion lie in the passions you had as a kid. For example, if you loved to make things maybe you should try an evening course, buy a sewing machine, or even join an art class; if you liked being outside, consider a new sport, getting fit or even running a race for charity.

And don't be fooled into thinking, 'what's the point?'. Suzanne, 26, was an avid reader as a kid and just let it slip as an adult. Three years ago, bored with frittering her spare time away on soap operas and drinks down the pub, she decided she was going to get back into reading again

24

EXERCISE FOUR

Brainstorm for a new life. Sit down with a pen and paper, and just list everything you'd like to do and be, places you'd like to go, skills you'd like to learn and personality traits you'd like to build on. It doesn't matter if your ideas are outlandish or if you really have no intention of ever doing them, the idea is to brainstorm so that you get used to the idea of keying into your desires and exciting yourself with the idea of what could be, instead of what is. If you're completely stuck, think about the things you loved as a kid, women you admire, lives you secretly covet and skills you wishfully want. Be bold about your choices, and when you have a list of about ten desires, focus on the details of your statements and what it would take to get there.

....

....

....

....

....

....

....

....

....

....

and picked up a book on living in Italy and found herself consumed with all things Italian. For the next year she took Italian lessons, learned to ski in Italy and spent every holiday in Italy. She even learned to cook Italian food. Of course, she eventually moved to Italy and now lives in Rome and is married to an Italian and is literally living la dolce vita.

For example: Kelly, 28, is a teacher who, in her own words, is currently, 'bored, single and overweight':

Desire 1: I want to fall in love and get married.
- **What's stopping me?**
  I never meet anyone.
- **What would get me there?**
  More dates, meeting new people, going to new places.
- **What can I do to change my life**
  Work less, make more of an effort to do things on my own, think of new avenues for dates such as Internet dating and asking around.

Desire 2: I want more excitement.
- **What's stopping me?**
  I can't think of what to do.
- **What would make my life more exciting?**
  Making new friends; taking more chances.
- **What would it take to achieve this?**
  Saying yes to more invites, joining in more and following through when I meet someone I like.

Desire 3: I want to lose weight.
- **What's stopping me?**
  No time or willpower.

- **What would get me there?**
  A better diet and more exercise.
- **What would it take to achieve this?**
  Join a gym and plan for healthy eating.

> **INSTANT NAUGHTY TASK**
> **Sign up for an evening class in something you've never done before and try it out at least twice in the next month. Possible ideas: yoga, creative writing, line dancing, belly dancing, drama, singing, martial arts, and so on.**

STEP FOUR

Save yourself

What are you really waiting for? A handsome rich guy who will sweep you off your feet and save you? A lottery win so that you can give up work and finally write that novel/film script or start a business? Enough savings so that you can finally pay off your debts and be the woman you've always wanted to be? Well, I hate to be the one to say it but love and money have never rescued anyone who hadn't already rescued herself, and although both help to make life more satisfying, neither will make you happy if you're unable to make yourself happy in the first place. If you don't believe me, see all the lottery winners whose lives go to pot after a substantial win, or the loved-up celebrities who still end up in expensive drying-out clinics.

The key to fulfilling your dreams and living a naughtier life is not to wait in the wings for the right circumstances to present themselves but to get out there, go for it and save yourself first. This entails a number of things, firstly a big kick in the pants to get you to change your ways, which is also known as scaring yourself into changing; a kick in the pants does what it says on the packet: it stops you procrastinating about why you can't do something and makes you do it. Of course, a self-administered kick is not the easiest thing to do because it entails imagining the worst-case scenario and using it to push yourself to change. But how you think and act today has very serious consequences on how you will live tomorrow. Stay put in your rut and in five years' time that's where you'll still be.

Secondly, stop moaning – and do something. Get used to doing something every day that works towards where you want to be. This means prioritise what it is that fills your heart with glee, and do it. Take this example of a friend of mine, who up until a few years ago was truly pathetic (she'd agree with this). She let men treat her badly, put up with a crap job with a bullying line manager and had a variety of friends who used her as a doormat. On top of this she griped constantly about how she hated living in the city and hated the stress of the rat race, until one day none of us could get hold of her. It turns out she decided she'd had enough and chucked in her job and went off travelling by herself. Drastic but true – this woman now lives in Australia where she is so happy it's nauseating. She's happily married, lives on the coast and can't believe she wasted so many years putting up with city life. Just one small step away from what she hated (well, a big step in her case) and she found everything else she wanted.

Which leads me to my last point: it is scary to go after your dreams and desires but it's worth doing even if you're afraid, because going after things you want will always be scary. Wanting something enough causes an adrenalin rush in the body and a natural feeling of fear and excitement. Ride it through, because it will pass and it is this that gets you to where you want to be.

'I always wanted to travel ever since I was about 12 years old but never really had the guts to do it, but when life got on top of me I finally did, and I found travelling alone gave me a huge amount of confidence and improved my self-esteem, as I experienced meeting new people/observing and comparing my life with others and learned how to have fun just for the sake of it. Bizarrely, I also found using the communal female showers at a music festival in South America a very affirming experience as we come in all shapes and sizes and realised it just doesn't matter what you look like!' Catherine, 29

EXERCISE FIVE

1. What would it take for you to take the stabilisers off your life?
2. What excuses do you tell yourself to stop you doing this?
3. Forget the worst thing that can happen, what's the best thing that can happen if you just go for it?

INSTANT NAUGHTY TASK
Take a step to fulfilling your wildest dream.

Desire rehab

GET READY AND GO

Quite simply, desire rehab is about putting what you've learned so far into action and making all those hidden dreams and desires a reality. Daunting though it may be to stand at the start of something new, it pays to view this time as something amazingly exciting and adventurous. You're on the way to change, you're daringly naughty, now all you have to do is go, go, go...

STEP ONE

Forget regrets

'It should have been me', is a popular refrain from a friend of mine who was once shortlisted for a film role that proved to be an Oscar winner for the actress who beat her to it. The actress is now ensconced in Beverly Hills with a life fresh out of the pages of a glossy magazine, whereas my friend is still tending a bar for a living and flat-sharing with three others, and saying, 'It should have been me'. While I can sympathise with her regrets, a large part of me wants to shake her and scream, 'MOVE ON', because it wasn't her, and in ten years my friend has spent more time focusing on losing that job than auditioning for new ones.

The reality is we all have regrets in life, whether it's turning down jobs or taking jobs, marrying or not, not taking our education further, taking our education too far. The list is endless and, if you allow them, your regrets can cause a huge pile-up in your life that will weigh you down and obstruct the road ahead – so just stop! Stop thinking about your regrets, stop worrying about what you could have done differently and stop being preoccupied with how rubbish and useless you are.

To put your desires into action you have to stop reminding yourself of all that's gone wrong before. Reliving failure means reliving the pain associated with it, instead of learning from what went wrong. Take Abi, 29, who has had a dream to write children's books all her life. She wrote one book five years ago, and ten agents and five publishers rejected it and she hasn't written a word since! Yet every time she talks about writing she talks about the pain and humiliation of the rejection. Dig deeper and it turns out every agent sent an accompanying letter telling her why her book wasn't right and suggested changes; yet, she hasn't considered a rewrite.

So ask yourself, what desires have you written off after one try? What's stopping you from searching out ways to make something work that you thought was impossible? How can you dig deeper and find new ways to make an old idea work for you?

INSTANT NAUGHTY TASK
Stop saying, 'Yes, but ...' and think of three ways to make one of your desires work right now.

EXERCISE ONE

List three things that went wrong before and track why it happened. Was it a lack of planning, a lack of support or a lack of determination that stopped your reaching your goal?

1. ....

....

2. ....

....

3. ....

....

List three new things you could do to make it work this time.

1. ....

....

2. ....

....

3. ....

....

STEP TWO

Get a mentor

A mentor is a person who can give you a helping hand with your life plans. Finding someone who has already been there and done that could well be your fast track to success and happiness. A good mentor is someone older with a broader vision than you, a person who sees something special in you, and above all has the ability to respect your dreams without rubbishing them. However, the trick is not just to attach yourself to the nearest successful diva but to identify someone you have an instant gut connection with. Get it wrong and you could end up caught in a power struggle like Hannah, 28, whose relationship with her mentor–boss soured when Hannah dared to go for a promotion that her boss had encouraged her against. This is why it's essential to think of someone you admire, someone who is successful in their own right and someone who is more happy than unhappy with their life.

On the whole your mentor should have a similar outlook to you, be the same sex (to avoid sex complicating matters) and be someone who has the ability to give help without taking over your life. If you can't think of the ideal person, then pay attention to what's going on around you. Look for friends who are raving about someone very wise, or look to see if you have a friend who has suddenly really grown with someone else's help.

More importantly, search for a person you admire, but are not wholly intimidated by and who genuinely likes you back. If there is no one who comes immediately to mind, think outside the box. Write to a famous businessperson, writer, and/or expert in your field and tell them you're looking for a mentor. Many successful people already know the benefits of mentoring and may even mentor already within set schemes so will be more willing to help than you might think.

Anna, 33, met her mentor when she was a wannabe writer in 1994. 'I went to a book-signing hoping to meet my favourite author, Isabelle Allende, but unfortunately about 500 other people had the same idea and I never even got to speak to her. But, I did start talking to the woman next to me, who also happened to be a writer, and over the years she has become my mentor. She was the one who urged me to carry on when my first book was rejected, and she's the one who I turn too when I feel I am wasting my time writing. She's what I need because, like me, she's struggling but has had a bit more success than me so she doesn't pussy-foot about, she tells it like it is especially when I feel like giving up, and I know she's what I need if I'm going to make it.'

Tough love is exactly what mentors are good at, as they take away your excuses and tell you to stop dreaming and to start making your dreams come true. You may not always want to hear what they say but you'll end up thanking them for their advice because you know that they're right. Which is why if you want a mentoring relationship to work, start by binning your defensive gene. Be open to criticism, it may make you feel sick inside when you hear something hard – but listen.

Find the right person and you should discover a whole new zest for life that goes beyond your age differences and your ambitions. The key is to not be afraid to seek out someone fantastic. Take the route of Yvonne, 32, who wooed a well-known fashion designer by email on a daily basis for two months until she agreed to be Yvonne's advisor–mentor on her end-of-year project. Or look at PR executive Kelly, 27, who called up her

EXERCISE TWO

- Think about who could be your mentor and why.
- Then send an email to them asking for help.

favourite teacher from school when she felt she was at a career and life dead end, and found herself with a perfect mentor. The relationship is about finding your way and being with someone who refreshes your view of the world. So choose someone who spurs you on and, above all, someone who persuades you to take crazy chances so that you can finally start living the way you've always dreamed you would.

INSTANT NAUGHTY TASK
Come up with three reasons why you'd be a good mentor to someone.

STEP THREE

Have an adventure

Let's face it, our daily lives are ruled by habits, which have most of us wandering around on autopilot. We eat the same foods, see the same people and go out to the same places; no wonder we wake up feeling bored and depressed with life. So if you want more excitement and bigger dreams it pays to have more adventures. Chasing a dream, going exploring and doing something outlandish can be a mind-blowing experience that will not only change you but also give you resources to draw on for the rest of your life.

Ten years ago, bored with life, one of my best friends decided it was time to have a big adventure. So she jacked in her very successful and glamorous job as a film PR, which she hated, gave up her Jimmy Choos, packed a large rucksack and bought a round-the-world ticket. At 28 everyone thought she was crazy to give up her life here to travel around the world, but she did it, and what's more she did it for two whole years until she met her Mr Right in Vietnam, caught a tropical disease in Australia and had to come home to recover. And recover she did, only to set off again with Mr Right to South America for two more years as soon as she got better. Eventually she did come home (just when we were beginning to think she'd disappeared for good) and settled down, got a job and had a baby (with Mr Right) because she said her adventure had become mundane and she was ready for a new one. These days if you met her you'd never know she

EXERCISE THREE

1. On your last holiday what changes did you say you would make when you got back?
2. What changes did you make, and if you didn't, which one could you make now?

had ridden elephants in Sri Lanka and climbed mountains in Peru, but she knows she did. She says she still uses the memories from that adventure whenever she feels she can't do something, as they encourage her to think back to when she was willing to be uninhibited, a little bit wild and a little bit crazy, and it helps her to reconnect with her desires and let go.

So my advice here: if you're looking to have fun as well as finding and fulfilling some hidden desires, break free of your schedule and shake yourself out of your current state with some adventures. And by adventures I mean ventures into something new. You can be like Diane, 30, who, post-break-up, spent a whole weekend jumping on the first train that came into a station and accidentally found a dream village in which to live. Or Kym, 28, who walks into any place, shop or café she finds interesting and talks to someone, no matter who they are. On the course of her adventures she's made two new friends, found a book group and dated a man. Dream endings aside, both women say the thrill of the ride and the accompanying confidence boost is what has made their ventures so worthwhile.

STEP FOUR

Stay inspired

How do you stay inspired by life when you're bored and your dreams seem a million miles away? Easy, you occupy your mind with things that make you think. Buying, shopping and manicures are not included, because whereas they fulfil the fun quota, no woman with real dreams would ever claim her number-one desire is to shop more! Constant shopping (and yes the Internet counts) and relationship talk are just diversions from doing something. So stop with the shopping and the boy talk and stay inspired by your plans.

How you do this is simple: shake up your spare time and spend less of it on the mundane and more of it on being crazily committed to new interests. Make whatever your dream is into a consuming passion for a while and fill your head with it, fill your time with it and focus your energies into it. By doing this you're guaranteed not only to have a higher chance of your dream becoming a reality but also you will have a higher chance of enjoying your life.

EXERCISE FOUR

1. What, or who, inspires you? Name three things?

a. ....

b. ....

c. ....

2. The next time you feel inspired, do something right away before the feeling of inspiration goes.

When I was single (and I was single on and off for a long time) I spent the great majority of my spare time talking about being single, moaning about being single and generally moping about being single. If a fantastic date had come into my life at that point, the truth is I would have had nothing to say to him apart from the woes of being single! Finally, when I saw my best friend's eyes glaze over yet again, and became utterly sick of the sound of my own voice, I decided that if I was going to be single then I was going to have the best single life ever and simply do whatever I wanted to do.

It was a liberating and inspirational thought because suddenly my time was not all focused on finding love (and complaining about dates) but actually about doing stuff, having fun and challenging myself with trivial obsessions just for the sake of it. I found it was exhilarating to let myself become hooked on something I found exciting, and for me that was exercise. So excited was I by the miraculous discovery that I actually liked to exercise that I didn't care what others thought of my new passion (most friends and family members just couldn't believe this was my chosen new passion). I didn't care if I had to do it on my own (previously I was the last person to do anything on my own) and I didn't care if I made an ass out of myself doing it, which I often do.

Over the years I have tried everything: climbing (impossible for me), yoga (hard but like it), kick-boxing (bruising but excellent), running (exhausting and love it), Pilates (bendy and love it), tennis (hate it with a passion), trampolining (why?), rollerblading (very humiliating), surfing (extremely humiliating!). The list is endless and I've loved every minute of it, and along the way I've found new business ideas, new friends and laughed a heck of a lot. While I am not suggesting exercise should be your consuming passion, seek out something equally trivial and enjoyable, get interested and you'll find yourself inspired by life all over again. None of us is made to be boring, we only become dull or bored because we give up and stop seeing what's out there for us.

INSTANT NAUGHTY TASK
Make it your goal to inspire a friend today, whether it's to try something new, go for a dream, take a chance or do something bold!

A word about desire and coupledom

Love conquers all – well not necessarily! If you're lucky you are with someone who's on the same desire wavelength as you; someone who wants to rev up their life, change things and live more dangerously – in which case, you can skip this section. Unfortunately, this isn't always the case. Take Jess, 33, who decided that after a lifetime of being overweight she wanted to be thin. For a year she dieted, exercised and whittled her body down by a staggering 38kg (84lb/6 stone)! Was her boyfriend happy? Well not quite, in fact he went out of his way to sabotage her weight loss, criticise her new look and then, when none of that worked, had an affair to make his point blindingly obvious; that is, his desire wasn't to see Jess become a sexy, happy and self-assured woman. Luckily, Jess was wise enough to see that they had conflicting desires, and happily moved on.

However, be warned: going after what you want isn't always this cut and dried in a relationship, and often you have to weigh up what you want and balance it against what you have, if you want to a happy outcome. Three years ago Catherine, 32, decided to act on her desire to travel the world, just as her fiancé's mother became ill. She went off alone and came back 18 months later realising her real desire was to get married, whereas her fiancé realised his real desire was to be with a woman who would stick around when he needed her. The moral of this story is that if you're attached to someone, think before you act on your desires. Meaning, communicate what you're doing. Work out if you're on the same wavelength and what to do if you're not, and above all talk, talk, talk about why you feel the need to do X and Y.

Of course, change is hard when you're watching someone you love changing, and it can be frightening and anxiety ridden, so if you intend to build a future together, here's how to tackle your new found enthusiasm for life and still stay happily together:

1. Be honest about your feelings for your current life, but also be sure to confirm that in looking for excitement and growth in your life you're not intending to grow away from your partner.
2. Ask your partner about his dreams and desires as well as telling him yours. What could you do together? How could you support each other and what adventures could you have together?
3. Consider if your partner is on your team; that is, is he supportive of your dreams and escapades or is he condemning? Tell him what you need from him.
4. Think about some joint desires that you could go after together – as the old saying goes: a couple who plays together, stays together.
5. Finally, are you heading in the same direction? Now that you want more, how does this fit into your current situation?

Freedom

MAKING YOUR DESIRES REAL

Once when I tried to encourage a work colleague to go for her dreams for a better career, she angrily said to me that the pleasure in dreaming about being an actress/writing a book/having her own million-dollar business (sorry I can't recall what it was but there was always some glamour angle to it) was just about the dreaming because it was an escape route and that's all. I'd have believed her if she wasn't someone who complained constantly about her life and how she was stuck, bored, held back and generally unable to do the things she wanted. She believed she used her dreams as an escape route, but actually all she was doing was torturing herself about her life and reminding herself constantly that it was not what she wanted it to be. The moral of this story is that it's fine to dream but if you never do anything with those dreams all you are doing is making your everyday reality miserable and not really living. So, either go after what you want, or make your dreams more frivolous and silly. If you want to make things come true, here's how to do it:

1. TAKE CHANCES TO HAVE MORE FUN

This is all part of saying yes to new things in your life. To have more fun, more excitement and definitely a sense of fun in your life you have to take chances. Date people who don't look good on the

packet, go places you once thought you'd never be seen dead in, and consider books, films, music and holidays you were once sure were definitely not you. You may be right, you may be wrong, but you will be surprised and this will increase your confidence, reboot your self-esteem and help you to take chances in making your desires real.

2. DO SOMETHING SILLY TO LIGHTEN UP

Having previously been someone who really didn't like to make a fool of herself, I have slowly learned the art of being silly just for the sake of it and the satisfaction that comes with it. This is thanks to my husband, who has no shyness when it comes to being a game for a laugh, as well as certain friends who have encouraged me to see that it doesn't really matter what others think. In my time I have ridden a bright red toy train round a park in Australia while lots of people watched, sang karaoke (extremely badly) and fallen off a trampoline. I previously thought making a fool out of myself in public would be the death of me, but discovered that really no one cares and, what's more, it makes people laugh. Best of all, lightening up has stopped me worrying about falling flat on my face, which in turn has freed me up to go after what I want.

3. HAVE A PLAN AND A TIME FRAME OR ELSE YOU'LL NEVER GET THERE

After years of talking about it, a friend recently chucked in her job, went for her dream and opened her own business over the space of two months, all because she simply stopped talking about it and started doing it. Which is why it pays to be a conscious do-er – that is, consciously take steps to make your desires real, don't just talk and don't just dream. You need a plan and a time frame or else this time next year you'll be exactly where you are now.

4. DO A LIFE AUDIT THREE TIMES A YEAR

(Also known as taking stock of how far you've come.) Sometimes when you're down it can be hard to see just how far you've made it and what changes you've made in yourself. Like weighing yourself to track if a diet is working, keeping a diary or doing regular life checks, this helps to remind you of what you're doing and where you want to be. Every four months, grab a notebook and have an afternoon for yourself. Ask yourself:

1. Am I happy – if not what would make me happier?
2. Am I doing what I want with my life – if not, how can I do it?
3. How far have I come in fulfilling my desires since the last audit?

5. TAKE RISKS

By this I mean take measured risks – that is, risks you can afford. Whereas jacking in your job, and running wild to get to your dreams is tempting, it's a road to ruin if you haven't worked out a way to pay your bills and your rent. Your aim is to put a plan into action, not do something drastic. Work out carefully what you're going to do, and the excitement and fulfilment will come from what you're doing, not what you've done.

6. EVERY DAY ASK YOURSELF: WHAT WAS BETTER ABOUT TODAY?

What might be better about today could be a sense of relief that you're finally underway, a sense of achievement that you managed to do something different or a feeling that you like getting up in the morning for the first time in years. This is also a way to focus on the positive rather than the stuff that went wrong or didn't happen.

Remember: what you give your attention to is what will increase and grow. Focus on how you're getting there and how you are changing, and that's what will keep happening.

7. MAKE TIME FOR YOUR DREAMS

Ask anyone what they're doing at the weekend and it's likely they'll come up with a list of domestic chores, social chores and shopping chores. Why? Well because our lives contain an infinite number of things we think we have to do, and this never changes, so what we have to do is make time by changing our attitude. Make a naughty to-do list every week of at least three things you actually want to do (these should be all the things you usually tell yourself you'll do when you have enough time) and then do everything on the list each week until it becomes second nature to relax, let go, have fun and go after what you want for a change.

TEN WAYS TO FULFIL YOUR DESIRES

1. Prioritise your desires and make a plan.
2. Have more adventures to widen your horizons and boost your confidence.
3. Challenge yourself to do things you're scared of – something once a week.
4. Do something out of character every day – just for the sake of it.
5. Every time you feel stuck, think about the woman you're becoming.
6. Ask for help or find a mentor.
7. Let go of your schedule and go with the flow.
8. Believe you can do it and forget the past.
9. Work out who's on your team.
10. Remind yourself of what you want from life and why.

One-month Desire Planner

The aim of the desire month planner is to take a step-by-step approach to changing your life by highlighting your hidden and not so hidden desires and working out how you can get from who you are now, to who you want to be.

Take at least ten minutes every day to consider each task.

WEEK ONE

Monday   Start a desire diary, which is for your eyes only and list three secret desires that you've never told anyone else about. These can be about your career, your love life, your hopes or making dreams come true. Don't censor yourself – focus on what you want from your life.

Tuesday   Spend ten minutes every day from now on (pick the same time every day to help create a habit) and think about YOU. That's what YOU want. What YOU need and what YOU have to do to change the parts of your life that you're not happy with.

Wednesday   Think reinvention. Focus on people you know and don't know i.e. famous people who have reinvented themselves, or made a come back and learn from their stories. Use the ones you admire as mentors for your own life. What do their stories teach you – what lessons can you take from them and make work in your own life?

Thursday   In today's ten minute YOU session differentiate between a daydream and a desire. Desires are rooted in some kind of reality whereas daydreams are not.

Friday   Do one thing today that moves you out of your comfort zone and closer to a desire. For instance if you want to meet a guy, go out and make an effort to flirt or at least smile at someone. If you're looking to move up the career ladder, speak to your boss about an idea, or about more responsibility. If you want a fresh start then sign up for a course.

Saturday   Rate your self-esteem out of ten. If you score seven or under think of three specific things that would improve the way you feel about yourself and put them into action whether it's something like a haircut, new wardrobe or a new skill.

Sunday	End the week with a new vision of who you are and where you are going. Spend an hour planning your new life, ensuring by the end of next week you'll have achieved three things on your to-do list.

WEEK TWO

Monday	Do something totally out of character at work today to show yourself how simple decisions can change your life. If you're stuck, try being positive all day about work and your colleagues! Note how people respond to you, how you respond to others and how you feel in general.
Tuesday	Spend the whole day living in the present. That's focusing on what you're doing right now, not what you're doing at lunch, after work, or at the weekend or in the summer. Every time you feel your attention drifting away, focus on your breathing to bring you right back into the present.
Wednesday	Think about how the people you love and like make you feel. Are you more optimistic in their presence, or more down-hearted? Who makes you feel as if you could do anything and who makes you judge yourself harshly? From this work out your team list i.e. the people who are 100 per cent on your side and those who aren't.
Thursday	Think about the last time you felt heady with excitement and literally jumped for joy. What activated that feeling? How could you recreate it and find it in your everyday life?
Friday	Tonight and this weekend do three new social things that you've never done before. Whether it's host a dinner party, go clubbing, see a film you'd never usually see or even go ice-skating. The aim is to broaden your horizons and challenge what you think your likes and dislikes are.

Saturday	Focus on your top desire and ask yourself what's stopping you from reaching it? Then brainstorm for ideas on how you could get from where you are now to where you want to be.
Sunday	Save yourself – as in stop waiting for a lottery win, Mr Right or a fantastic new job to change your life – instead change it yourself by taking the right steps to get to what you want. If you're stuck then ask for help, research on the Internet and take some risks.

WEEK THREE

Monday	Ask yourself what you can learn from your biggest mistakes and then write a list to remind yourself what not to do ever again.
Tuesday	Forget your regrets for good. Spend 30 minutes writing down everything you feel guilty about and what you regret and then without re-reading your list, rip it into tiny pieces and bin it. What's past is literally past so there's no point holding on to it and letting it drag you down.
Wednesday	Drop your schedule for a day, be really naughty and take the day off. Then for the whole day do whatever you want. That means whatever takes your fancy, and whatever you feel like doing. It's a YOU day.
Thursday	Inspire yourself. It's easier to dream bigger if you broaden your horizons. So for the rest of the month indulge in different books, new music, art for art's sake, films you've never watched and sport you've never tried and see where it takes you.
Friday	Lighten up for a whole day and don't worry about what people think about you, and just act on gut instinct. If you feel like doing it – do it!

Saturday	Have an adventure, whether this entails going along to a station and jumping on the first train heading out or walking into a restaurant and trying a type of cuisine that's so 'not you'. Whatever you choose make sure it's something that tests your boundaries and takes you out of your comfort zone.
Sunday	Make 'have more fun', your new motto so that whatever you do your first question should always be, 'Am I having fun?'. If you're not, ask yourself why you're doing it and for whose sake.

WEEK FOUR

Monday	Open your mind to new possibilities and desires. What other desires can you incorporate into your life to boost your confidence and your self-esteem?
Tuesday	Time frame two desires so that they don't just become dreams that you think you'll do one day soon. Work towards them or else take them off your list.
Wednesday	Have your first life audit – this is where you run through everything in your life and work out what's working well, what you love, what you need to improve and what you need to cull from your life.
Thursday	Focus on the good. Note how much better you feel about your life now you're travelling in the direction of your desires. Have you become more positive? Has your self-esteem grown? What's the best result of your changes?
Friday	Keep believing you can be who you want to be even if you've experienced a setback or found that the road ahead was rockier than you thought. You've come this far, don't give up now.
Saturday	Don't be afraid to change lanes, meaning if your desire runs out of steam, don't be afraid to change it or focus on some-

thing new. Desires aren't written in stone and are only worth going for if they are what you want above all other things.

Sunday   Stay watchful of old habits sliding back in. It's tempting to return to form but remember how you felt when you put your desires on hold. Don't let that happen again.

Attitude

Introduction

Attitude counts in the naughty-girl stakes, not because I'm trying to turn you into a pushy diva ready to throw everyone aside to get what she wants, but because if you're hoping to get what you want in life, you have to start by changing the way you think and act. Attitude drives behaviour; meaning, hate yourself and/or believe you were born to fail and have a boring life and your behaviour will drive you in that direction. Think small and believe you're worthless, and that's what you'll get, which is why finding a naughty attitude is simply about turning up the volume in your life and living a louder life that shouts that you're here, ready and able.

'But I have a good attitude', I hear you cry, 'I'm always doing stuff for others and putting others' needs before mine!'. Well, of course, caring is good, but if you're being good to cover up your needs or because you need to be needed, it's not a good attitude you have but good-girl syndrome! This is where you suck back your own desires and pleasures, act nice when you really don't feel like being nice, and do what others want, because you want to be liked. Whereas having a naughty attitude is better, because it's about having a great, fantastic and unbelievably wonderful attitude about yourself (that's attitude not ego) that makes you want to live a better life and be better in your life.

A naughty attitude is about having the attitude that we had as kids. The one where we'd choose to do something even though we knew there was a risk that we would get caught, hurt or maybe fall flat on our face because we knew the chances for having the time of our lives were staggeringly high. Cultivate a naughty-but-nice attitude like this in your adult life and you won't be someone who thinks you're lucky to be where you are because you're actually a bit untalented or lucky to be given work and you're faking it and lucky to have such a wonderful boyfriend because he's so much nicer than you! Instead, you'll be someone who believes in what she's doing, isn't afraid to say what she wants, and isn't afraid to change direction a little (or a lot). Once this happens you'll be able to give your own needs as much attention as everyone else's, which means you will have more time doing what you want, more fulfilment in what you do, and more personal happiness all round.

Best of all, girls with a naughty-but-nice attitude go far in life because they're nobody's fool. If you're already flagging over this attitude adjustment and wondering if it really matters, educate yourself. The world is full of powerful examples of women who got themselves an attitude and then a life; women who were mistreated by loved ones and found the attitude to say 'STOP'; women who were harassed at work and did something about it; and women who were told by their communities that they were worthless because of their sex, skin colour or even how much money they earned, and then changed people's views. Your own personal change doesn't have to carry the same impact of how these women changed their attitude and the world's, but you can learn from their example, because once you have a strong attitude like them, you'll never look back.

> 'My confidence, strength and attitude has saved me from three bad relationships in my past. In all three cases I suffered from domestic violence and was blamed for the abuse because I 'always wanted to do stuff' or was 'too strong' or simply because I wouldn't let them control me. My self-esteem, although battered at times, has survived thanks to my attitude that I deserve more from life.' Sarah, 32

Quiz

WHAT'S YOUR ATTITUDE RATING?

Are you one of life's louder people, known for hollering out the injustices thrown your way on a daily basis? Or are you a suffer-in-silence kind of girl looking for a quiet life with no hassles? Try this quiz to score where you land on the attitude scale.

1. **You're standing in line when a smarter, older woman pushes in front of you and gets served first. What do you do?**
   a. Say as politely as possible: 'Excuse me, I was first.' (B)
   b. Say as loudly as possible: 'EXCUSE ME' and then accuse the shop assistant of favouritism. (A)
   c. Say nothing but seethe with anger. (C)
   d. Ignore it; it happens all the time to you. (D)

2. **A friend informs you that despite your best efforts to get fit and lose weight, you're clearly not the slim type. What do you do?**
   a. Agree that you're rubbish and will be chubby for life. (D)
   b. Agree but silently decide to strike her off your friendship list forever. (C)
   c. Get really angry with her. (A)
   d. Disagree but feel upset. (B)

3. **At work your boss ignores your input in a project you've worked really hard on and thanks everyone but you. You take it as a sign that:**
a. You've offended him. (C)
b. He's threatened by your talent. (A)
c. He doesn't think much of your input. (B)
d. It's somehow your fault. (D)

4. **The heel on a new pair of boots breaks the first time you wear them, so you take them back to a shop but they refuse to refund your money. You:**
a. Stand your ground even though you're uncomfortable, because you know you're right. (B)
b. Shout loudly until a manager comes and you get your way. (A)
c. Accept their view and leave feeling mistreated. (D)
d. Accept an exchange instead but feel bad. (C)

5. **Your friend borrows your best dress and returns it in a nasty condition promising to get it cleaned when she has the money. You:**
a. Say 'don't worry' and get it cleaned yourself so that at least you know it's done. (C)
b. Get angry and insist she buys you a new dress right away. (A)
c. Feel gutted but allow her to get it cleaned. (B)
d. Somehow end up apologising. (D)

6. **A guy you are dating says something you really disagree with. What do you do?**
a. Agree to disagree, as you don't want to fall out with him. (B)
b. Consider that maybe you're wrong because he looks like he knows more than you. (D)

c. Argue it out with him – as you know he's wrong. (A)

d. Don't tell him you disagree because you hate confrontations. (C)

7. **You go up for a job, and when you arrive you find yourself in a room of women the same age as you. How do you feel when you look around?**

a. Gutted because they all look smarter and prettier than you. (C)

b. Ready to leave, because what's the point, you'll never get this job. (D)

c. Annoyed that you've landed in what feels like a cattle market; you know your CV makes you stand out. (A)

d. Nervous because you're unsure how you're going to make the right impact. (B)

8. **You're in a relationship but you want out because you've met someone new, but your boyfriend is so nice, what do you do?**

a. Behave badly until your boyfriend gets so sick of you he ends it. (B)

b. Have an affair behind his back and leave clues so that he finds out. (A)

c. Stay with him because you hate to hurt him. (D)

d. End it but feel so guilty you refuse to date anyone new. (C)

9. **A pushy shop assistant is eager to sell you a pair of shoes you feel don't suit you. What do you do?**

a. Promise you'll definitely come back later and then feel bad for not doing so. (C)

b. Buy them because she probably knows more than you about shoes. (D)

c. Say no, but overdo your gratitude for her help. (B)

d. Accuse her of thinking more about her commission than you and vow never to come back again. (A)

10. **Your boyfriend says he is leaving you and claims it's your fault, and then lays a list of your faults at your feet. What do you do?**
a. Cry – you had no idea you'd been getting him down. (D)
b. Beg him to reconsider and say you'll improve. (C)
c. Turn on him and list all his many, many faults. (A)
d. Say 'go, then' – and then feel horrible about yourself. (B)

Results

Add up all the answers you gave that were followed by (A) and then those followed by (B), and so on. Then see which score was the highest. If you scored highest on the (A) answers that means you have a Bad Attitude, see below. If you scored highest on the (B) answers that means you have a Self-doubting Attitude, and so on.

BAD ATTITUDE (mostly As)

Well, you certainly have an attitude, but if you've ever wondered why it's not helping you in life it's because it's an attitude fuelled by insecurity and anger and not by confidence. Meaning, you lash out and overreact when you feel you're being cheated, treated like a fool and taken advantage of. Whereas it's good to be responsive to people who hit your wrong buttons, your attitude is not allowing you to make the right assumptions about situations, which means you often overreact because you've misread someone's signals or get aggressive when you'd be better off being assertive. The good news is that boosting how you see yourself will make the small adjustment needed in your attitude to start turning things around in your life.

SELF-DOUBTING ATTITUDE (mostly Bs)

You have half an attitude, which means you have the guts to react when people take advantage of you, and you stand up for yourself, but you don't have the confidence to follow through effectively. This means you need to be 100 per cent bolder with your reactions so that you get the response you're looking for. To do this you need to boost your self-esteem and, once you feel more sure of yourself, you'll be less afraid of what others think and not embarrassed about standing up for what you believe in. The good news is you have the words already so all you need to do is think about how to back this up with good body language and tone, as it's these things that help create a strong and don't-mess-with-me attitude.

BOTTLED-UP ATTITUDE (mostly Cs)

Somewhere deep inside you is an attitude desperate to get out, and you know it, but what's keeping it down is your low self-esteem. You give people – whether they are your boss, friends or partners – more power than they deserve and so feel weak in their presence, which in turn leaves you unable to stand up for yourself. The good news is you are aware that your attitude is bottled up and you do want to be braver – and you can be. To do so, you need to uncork your feelings and allow yourself to feel all the not-so-nice emotions that you quash, such as anger, frustration, annoyance and irritation.

FRAGILE ATTITUDE (mostly Ds)

Currently your self-worth and self-belief are riding so low that you're letting everyone walk all over you. I say currently, because somewhere back in time you did have an attitude that wasn't based on the belief that you're rubbish and deserve to be treated badly. Repeat after me: 'I am worthy', it's not always your fault, you don't always have to believe what other people say, and you don't have to apologise all the time! The good news is your attitude is currently so low that the only way for you is up!

Attitude
FACING THE FACTS

If you're stuck in a rut, bored, sad or you feel that there's just no point in trying any more, your attitude definitely needs a rescue remedy, and the good news is that despite how low you're feeling right now, inside each and every one of us is a better attitude waiting to be sprung. This is because our attitude isn't set in stone (even if it sometimes feels that way) but is actually an ever-changing state of mind that we control. Partly formed by our beliefs, past experiences, and perception of the world, our attitude is also based on conscious reaction; that is, the way we choose to react to the things that happen to us. This is why some people can go through terrible times and come out saying it was the best thing that ever happened to them, whereas others are floored by smaller things and can't get back up.

What's all this got to do with getting what you want? Well, simply put, a bad, negative and stagnating attitude acts against you, because it affects behaviour, which in turn stops you from going for what you want out of life. Meaning, if you want to stand up and be counted, finally get the kudos you feel you deserve and have the guts to go after the things you want in life you have to cultivate an attitude that encourages you to go after these things. Don't be like Amy, 28, who has an 'I'm not worthy' attitude about her relationships that leave her stuck with losers who take advantage of her; or Emma, 26, who will listen intently to ideas on how she can get past her domineering manager and get promoted, but then will give you a hundred reasons why nothing will work. Emma's boss is not so powerful that her staff are powerless against her, and Amy's boyfriends are not so amazing that she'd be stupid to leave, but both women have attitudes that ensure they stay exactly where they are. So it's time to take a long, hard look at your mind power and work out if your attitude is for you or against you.

STEP ONE

WARNING – bad attitude ahead!

Define a person with a bad attitude and you'll probably think of someone with a chip on their shoulder; a person who lashes out at the world because they can't take responsibility for their actions and behaviour; and/or someone who is angry, aggressive and pushy because they feel cheated by life. Whereas that's one type of bad attitude, a bad attitude can and does take many other forms, too, such as:

- The person who's always self-deprecating and down on herself.
- The person who always puts others before herself no matter what.
- The person who worries so much about what could go wrong that she's immobilised by fear.
- The person who worries too much about what others think and so doesn't do anything.

The list of variations on bad attitudes is endless, and even if you don't fit into one of the above, you will know if your attitude needs an adjustment because either someone else has politely (or not so politely) told you or you're getting to the stage where you're beginning to realise you're your own worst enemy.

Take Kathy, 28, who blames the fact she's 6.4kg (14lb/1 stone) overweight on her job and working hours: 'I really want to lose weight but I don't have any time to get to the gym because of work, and they never serve healthy food in the café there, so I don't get a choice what to eat and always end up snacking on chocolate. Then there's the biscuit tin they have by the coffee machine. It's like they want you to put on weight. In another company I'd be slim, I know I would be.'

Or Hayley, 27, who blames her boyfriend because she hasn't pursued what she wanted in life. 'Before I met Matt, I wanted to be a singer. I had a good voice and wanted to go for it, but meeting Matt was distracting and he wasn't that into music, so I gave it up to be with him. Now I am stuck at home bored and doing nothing while he's out doing something he likes. I want to change things but I don't know what.'

On the surface both Hayley and Kathy say they are eager for things to change, but the reality is that nothing will until they change their attitude about how they ended up where they are today. Blaming others (even if it actually is the fault of others), seeking solutions outside of yourself and waiting for things to happen are all ways of ensuring your attitude stays the same and nothing changes. To get from where you are now to where you want to be you have to work on an attitude overhaul by (1) taking responsibility for all your decisions and mistakes; (2) learning from the things that went wrong in your life; and (3) moving on.

EXERCISE ONE

1. Think of three times when your attitude has acted against you.

a. ....

b. ....

c. ....

2. List three times when your attitude has worked in your favour.

a. ....

b. ....

c. ....

3. What was the difference in your attitude between (1) and (2)?

....

....

....

....

....

....

The main way to improve your attitude is to improve your self-esteem – or rather how you feel about yourself. Of late self-esteem has been given a bad press, but the truth is it's an essential and vital component of a good attitude (and a good life) because when you feel great about yourself and really believe you are worth something, your attitude tends to ride high alongside. This in turn affects your behaviour and makes things start to happen.

In case you're worried, contrary to popular belief, self-esteem has nothing to do with inflated egos and arrogance. If anything, the people with the best esteem don't have colossal egos because they know they don't have to shout loudly about themselves to get noticed or to make things happen. Large egos, on the other hand, tend to come from people who feel some-what inferior and so constantly have to prove to people that they are better than everyone else.

Steps to boosting your self-esteem are simple. Start valuing your skills and your talents, and before you even say, 'but I have no skills/good points/talents' and so on, be aware that everyone has something to offer, and if you don't believe me sit down with two valued friends and write a list of what you perceive to be your best points, and list everything no matter how inconsequential you may feel these things are.

For example: Anna, 28, who is an accounts officer but would like to work in the food industry, wrote the following on her list:

Best points
I'm good at my job
I'm an okay cook
I'm a nice friend

Anna's friends, Steph and Lisa, amended her list this way:

- Anna is great at her job but she's too clever for it and bored by it, but she won't be convinced to go for something more.
- Anna is a fabulous cook and a really creative one – she even won a cooking competition, but she won't take it further no matter what we say.
- Anna is a brilliant friend, good at listening and helping. She always puts us before her own needs – she's more than nice.

It doesn't take an expert to see that Anna's lack of self-worth means she can't bring herself to value her skills as skills because she assumes that if she finds something easy or it's second nature then it's not a skill. This in turn not only stops her from believing what anyone says to encourage her but also keeps her in a lowly job and makes her feel disillusioned with her dreams. And that's the problem with having a low attitude about yourself: you're in a continual lose-lose situation. You can't be positive about yourself or your skills, so you can't allow anyone else to be positive about you, and yet you desperately want someone to prove to you that you are someone worth valuing and so end up dissatisfied and unhappy. If Anna's story rings a bell, here's how to start improving your self-esteem:

1. SPEND LESS TIME THINKING ABOUT YOURSELF

It sounds strange, but low self-esteem is often accompanied by too much focus on the self. If you find that you are thinking yourself into a negative spiral all the time and listing your bad points, lack of life, and so on, and why you don't deserve more, you need to do something that absorbs your mind and holds your attention away from your woes (see Desire section for more on this).

2. REMEMBER YOUR ACHIEVEMENTS

Put together a mental list of self-esteem-boosting memories, and if you're thinking 'but I've never achieved anything', pick things that made you feel heady with joy and pleasure, like falling in love, losing weight, passing an exam, learning to swim, playing sport, or helping a friend.

3. CHANGE SOMETHING ABOUT YOURSELF

If you feel you are just a reflection of what your parents and friends want you to be, reinvent yourself. If you're feeling desperate to express yourself, change something: your look, what you do in your social time, or even how you speak up at work.

4. FORGET ABOUT PERFECTION

Mr Right, more money, a bigger house, a tiny bottom, hair that doesn't frizz, and breasts that are bigger/smaller/more pert – if these are just some of the must-haves on your perfection wish list, think again. Waiting for perfection in order to be happy is a delaying tactic to avoid going after what you want, and it's a guaranteed way to keep your esteem down (for more on this see the section on Sexiness).

'I'm not preoccupied with how others view me; however, I am aware that family and friends would be disappointed if I became scruffy or were unlipsticked; they would be concerned that something was wrong. I almost feel I have a duty not to let them down. This now sounds completely egotistical but I know I am considered to be eccentric by my family, and this doesn't offend me at all – it's just who I am!' Anita, 30

5. ACCEPT COMPLIMENTS

Or rather, learn to take them graciously. People aren't just being 'nice' or saying it because 'they have to'. If you keep batting the good remarks away because you think people are lying, you're actually teaching people that it's not okay to praise you.

6. MAKE YOUR WEAKNESSES YOUR STRENGTHS

So you're too soft, or too quiet, or too loud, or too silly – these might feel like weaknesses but they can also be your strengths. Look for a spin on the negative emotion for instance: too soft means you're sensitive and intuitive; too quiet means you're a good listener; and too loud means you like to stand up for yourself.

7. HAVE A PLAN

Most people with low self-esteem don't have goals or a plan on how to reach their goals so they always feel stuck. To change how you feel about yourself start charting the change you find in yourself: keep a diary; set long- and short-term goals; and give yourself a life audit to see where you're going and why.

> **INSTANT NAUGHTY TASK**
> **Look in the mirror and, without thinking, say three things out loud that you love about yourself. Don't think just do it.**

STEP TWO

Live for now

For a moment let go of your present attitude and stop telling yourself all the reasons why you can't get to where you want to be in life. While you're at it, forget what you have or haven't done, the things you did wrong along the way, why you could kick yourself for not grabbing opportunities as they arose, and why you hate your body/thighs/stomach.

Whereas it's good to know where you came from (and why) and fantastic to know where you want to go and who you want to be, it's your present attitude that counts. So think about what you do right now every day to build up your attitude about yourself. What do you say to yourself when you look in the mirror, how do you feel when you face your work, speak to friends, or even just sit on the bus? And more importantly, ask yourself how would you feel if an opportunity to get what you want was presented to you right now? Would you grab it? Procrastinate over it? Feel it was too good to be true or ignore it because if it's meant to happen it will? It's your response to the above that should show you how your attitude today is building your life for tomorrow.

If you feel disillusioned all the time, this is a defeatist attitude. Getting rejected, failing when you try, falling flat on your face and having your hopes dashed are the ways most of us learn to give up, stop trying and start thinking: 'That's it – what's the point? This is as good as it gets.' Yet it's important to see that it's not the failing that stops us getting what we want but the 'what's the point?' attitude that ultimately stops us from trying again to get what we want. So the next time you feel your attitude flagging in defeat, think of the author J.K. Rowling who went through numerous rejections before someone bought *Harry Potter*, or the motivational speaker Susan Jeffers whose world-famous book *Feel the Fear* was rejected about 80 times before someone snapped it up, or even Olympic winner Kelly Holmes who was told that, at 34 years old, she was past it, and then went on to win two gold medals in the 2004 Olympics. My point here is that while it's normal and understandable to be disappointed when plans fail, having a disillusioned attitude is a trap that will shut you in a dead-end job/relationship for life.

If you procrastinate all the time, this is a non-doing attitude. Meet Sara, 28, who is desperate to move to Australia and has wanted to do this since she was 19 when she returned home from her gap year. Nearly ten years have passed and Sara has yet to research the basics of how to emigrate, despite constantly talking of moving, and although she can list 100 reasons why Australia is the place for her. 'My problem is I'm lazy', says Sara, but the reality is she procrastinates because she's afraid to move and no longer sure what she wants, which means she's stuck because she has a conflicted attitude about her life plans. If you're one of life's great procrastinators you need to stop talking and start doing! Big talkers like Sara rarely have big attitudes about themselves, and instead fail to achieve their goals simply because all their energy is spent discussing rather than doing and thinking about why their plans haven't taken off.

If you feel good things only happen to others, this is a safety-net attitude. If you tell yourself that good things don't happen to people like you, then what you're actually doing is giving yourself permission to not try, not hope for more under the guise of never being disappointed. Take Catherine, 30, who's given up dating because she says, 'I know that I'm not one of those lucky people who end up falling in love so I made a decision not to date any more and it's fine. I don't get to feel hurt and rejected and I feel more in control of what I do. It's not the same as giving up'. Sadly, it *is* the same as giving up!

If you believe things will happen if they are fated to, this is an 'I have no control' attitude. Believing that your life is predestined and that if things are meant to happen they will is a dangerous attitude to adopt because you run the risk that nothing whatsoever will happen to you. Things happen in life (both good and bad) not because they are predestined but because you make choices, and doing nothing is a very big choice. So if you feel your life is stuck and that fate has dealt you a bad hand, take responsibility for what you have or haven't done and take back the control.

EXERCISE TWO

To help yourself locate what kind of attitude you have and why,
ask yourself:
1. What positive and negative messages were you given about your attitude when growing up?
2. When you did or said something bold and confident as a child, how did your parents respond?
3. Did your parents have differing attitudes to life?
4. How did your parents respond when things went wrong?
5. Can you think of a defining moment that changed your attitude completely?

Then to see how your attitude works, ask yourself:
1. Does your current attitude reflect your mother's view on life, your father's or neither?
2. List two reasons why your attitude works against you.

a. ....

b. ....

3. List two ways in which your attitude positively benefits you.

a. ....

....

b. ....

....

4. What could you do to improve your attitude right now?

....

....

....

....

....

....

....

....

....

INSTANT NAUGHTY TASK

Change your attitude for just one day and act in a way you are usually too afraid to act in. For example, be bold if someone asks for your opinion, say yes to an offer you usually turn down, or volunteer for work you usually wait to be asked to do, and see how it makes you feel.

STEP THREE

Change your focus

Okay it's time to stop being a self-fulfilling prophecy of the negative kind and start remembering you're only as lucky as your expectations expect you to be. Meaning, start believing you're worth something and you'll start getting that something on a regular basis. Of course, it's hard to believe and focus on your worth, when as women we are bombarded on a regular basis with pictures and articles about why we're not perfect the way we are and how we need to be perfect to get by in this life. And by perfect we're told we have to be young, slim and wrinkle-free – as shown by the multitude of TV reality programmes showing us how to get a perfect makeover of the plastic-surgery kind. The best way to handle these images, stories and programmes is literally to switch off from them. As enjoyable as it may be to see a famous person's cellulite, these stories are brainwashing you into thinking you're not good enough, and the truth is you are!

The key is to think about what you want in life, not what someone else is telling you that you want. Then think about what you tell yourself about these things every day. Take Sara, 24, who says she has had a 'serious fat attitude' since she was 15 years old. Sara weighs in at 76kg (168lb/12 stone) and wants to lose around 12.7 kg (28lb/2 stone) to become her 'perfect' weight. At this weight Sara believes she will get what she wants: 'Men will ask me out, I'll get to go to travelling and I can join a gym.' The ironic thing is that Sara does get asked out, she could join a gym right now and she could go travelling. What's stopping her is her attitude. She doesn't say yes to any of her dates because she can't believe men find her attractive, and that is because she doesn't find herself attractive. She won't go travelling because she feels she physically won't be able to until she's slim and she won't join a gym because she believes they are only for fit people.

On the other hand, take Emma, 33, who at 82.6kg (182lb/13 stone) has done all of the above as well as run a marathon and climbed a mountain and found her Mr Perfect. She's heavier than Sara, yet when you speak to her she has the zest of a woman half her size. The difference between these two women is that Emma's attitude carries her forward because she believes she can do things, and Sara's attitude doesn't. Of course, we all know that like Sara's mind, the brain will wander down any scary, self-defeating alley you allow it to, which means the only way to stop feeling you can't do things in life and can't get the things you want is literally to STOP THINKING YOU CAN'T DO IT!

'I know several women with high self-esteem and fantastic attitudes about themselves. I think they have what I would call contagious positive energy and you want to be around them. They make you feel as if you can achieve anything and never take no for an answer.' Jane, 27

It's pointless to assume you are always going to be the person who will get the raw end of the deal, and comfort yourself with the thought that at least you're 'honest' about your shortcomings and failings. The reality is, believing you are worse off than everyone else and that no tactic will work for you, is incredibly self-involved and egotistic because what you're really saying is that the strategies that work for other people just won't work for you because your case is unique and special. Sorry, but it's not. Whereas details differ, all of us have had times when we felt stuck, frustrated, weighed down and squashed by life, and when this happens you have my sympathy, but you also need to get to a point where you say, 'enough', and get on with things.

What you want in life is attainable; some things may take more work, risks and challenges than others, but on the whole you have as much chance at being happy, contented and excited as the next person.

How can it be this simple? Well, negative thinking is a habit, and like all habits it's broken by a decision to stop, and while stopping the misery record that goes on in your head may seem like a small change it's one that will have a large impact on your future. Just modify your assumptions about yourself by a tiny degree by assuming things will work out for a change and watch the domino effect it will have on the rest of your life.

EXERCISE THREE

To see where you place your focus ask yourself:
1. When you look in the mirror what do you focus on? Good points, bad points?
2. When someone gives you a compliment, what's your first thought?
3. If someone asks you to do something new and scary – what's your most likely reaction?
4. When you meet someone new what's the first thing you focus on about him or her?

INSTANT NAUGHTY TASK

Think about your naughty aims – more fun, more adventure, better self-worth and self-esteem – at least four times a day. This teaches you to refocus on what you want, no matter what kind of day you're having. Have set times to do this: when you get up, at lunch, on the way home from work and before you go to bed.

STEP FOUR

Take more risks

The number-one way to improve your attitude and gain a naughtier life is to start taking risks, and by risks I don't mean doing a reckless, death-defying stunt that brings you close to harm, but taking risks that bring you closer to what you want. These kinds of risks feel scary, and when I say feel scary I mean they feel uncomfortable, they make your heart race and may even make you feel a little sick. This is normal so don't worry, because by taking a risk and upping your chance of failure and/or rejection your body and mind will rebel at first (plus, let's face it, excitement is actually an adrenalin rush to the head). And as the old saying goes: no pain, no gain!

You won't get anything in life without putting yourself on the line. Want to find Mr Right, fall in love and live happily ever after? Well, you need to risk dating. Want to be your own boss, spend your days working for yourself and earn lots of money? Well, you have to risk financial failure to get there. Want to have more adventures, do naughtier things and live it up? Well you need to risk embarrassment and maybe falling on your face to get it.

The good news is that risk-taking, although scary, isn't hard. Once you get used to feeling a certain layer of discomfort, your confidence will build up. One way to get used to this and to avoid it overwhelming you and stopping you in your tracks is to understand fear and what it does to the body. Fear is the unknown, the uncontrollable, the danger hiding in dark corners, and the key to beating it is to trust that it won't squash you. When you take a risk, adrenalin is released by the brain in response to what it perceives to be a stressful situation, and even if you're about to do something that you really want to do, the brain will still perceive it as stress in order to help you to find the energy to cope with it. When this happens you will feel an increase in your heart rate and pulse rate, and it also raises your blood pressure – making you feel hot, sweaty and ready for what's known as fight or flight: that is, stay and face it or run away.

The good news is that when you take a risk, adrenalin actually makes you stronger, faster and even gives your body the ability to absorb more pain than it normally would. This is to help you get through the event – not stop you from doing it. Things to remember are:

- **Everybody feels fear and gets a rush of adrenalin when doing something new. Feeling like this is perfectly natural and does not mean that you're doing the wrong thing.**
- **People often freeze when their body releases adrenalin because they are not used to the feeling and they mistake it for panic.**
- **Adrenalin is there to help you, not hinder you, but you need to utilise it quickly by taking action; that is, going for it. Your adrenalin will be used powerfully in your favour if you choose to act quickly.**

TYPES OF ADRENALIN RELEASED BY FEAR

Slow-release adrenalin when thinking about taking a risk. This happens when you know something scary is approaching, such as a date you're anxious about, something new you're about to try, or the date you leave or start a job. When a future risk is in view the body will release small amounts of adrenalin over several days as the scenario gets closer.

Adrenalin release due to thinking about consequences. Adrenalin is also released if you think about the negative consequences of a risky event. This has its uses, as it may lead you to decide not to go through with a particular risk because you don't want it after all, or to approach it in a different way.

Quick adrenalin release as you do something risky. This is known as an adrenalin dump and happens when a large quantity of adrenalin is instantly released into the body as the result of an immediate action. This is the most common adrenalin release but very powerful. Your mind will recognise something as threatening and your body will release a large amount of adrenalin to help you.

YOUR BODY'S RESPONSE TO TAKING A RISK

Again, it's worth knowing how adrenalin affects your body so that you're not shocked when you feel it sweeping through your parts:

- Body or limbs shaking.
- Palms of the hands become sweaty.
- Your mouth becomes dry.
- Your voice becomes high pitched and/or has a tremor.
- You feel physically sick.

- You feel a need to go to the toilet.
- Time distorts and events happen really quickly or very slowly.
- Your heart beats faster to supply blood to your muscles.

EXERCISE FOUR

1. Risk something new today – it can be speaking up, speaking out, wearing bright colours, and so on.
2. Note how the risk makes you feel.
3. What have you learned about yourself from taking the risk?

The good new is that the more risks you take, the more resilient you become to fear and adrenalin surges, setbacks, embarrassment and other blocks that stop you from heading out there and doing what you want. This means you will empower yourself, have more of a devil-may-care attitude, and find yourself brimming with self-confidence.

INSTANT NAUGHTY TASK
Decide on one frivolous thing you have always wanted to do.
It can be joining a gym/dating agency/evening class or asking a man out, getting your hair dyed, even pole-dancing or buying a sexy pair of knickers. Then just do it!

Attitude rehab

PUTTING YOUR NEW ATTITUDE INTO ACTION

Now you know what it takes to create a better attitude, it's time to put it into action and let your attitude drive your behaviour. Remember: whatever you focus on and believe in (both negatively and positively) is what you'll be driven towards. So put yourself in control of your time, and your life and set goals towards being the person you want to be, using your new-found attitude as a guide. The key is to prioritise what you want, not overwhelm yourself with a list, and focus on the naughty/serious balance you want in each area of your being: work, yourself and life.

STEP ONE

Better attitude, better life

Girls with a healthy attitude to life simply care less about what others think and more about what they think. Of course, it's a hard one, especially if you're a people-pleaser who gets rewards from making others happy. However, placing your happiness in someone else's hands is always bad news because it leaves you at their mercy.

Take Marie, 28, who, as she says, 'Used to be the kind of person who wouldn't get up and dance at a club or party because I was afraid of what others would say about me. I was always afraid of being judged by people and afraid they'd think I wasn't good enough or cool enough.' What changed Marie was the realisation that everyone else was out there having a good time and she wasn't. 'I just realised it one day. I was sitting at this dance club feeling all uptight and awkward as usual, and I suddenly thought – everyone is having a good time but me, so it can't be their problem but mine. It changed my attitude in an instant.'

If, like Marie, you want to move from a meek life to an dynamic one, start by realising that meek living is where you sit back and wait for life, love and opportunities to come to you and then when they don't you complain about your lack of luck, being bored and feeling frustrated. Dynamic living, on the other hand, is where you take control of your destiny and make your life move.

> 'They key to a better attitude truly is to spend less time thinking about yourself. I know this because I spent years talking about how I wanted to get married but didn't have a boyfriend, about how I wanted to be thinner but couldn't lose weight and how I hated myself because I was boring and dull and couldn't get those things. Now I realise I couldn't get those things because all I was doing was being completely me-focused. No wonder no one ever asked me out.' Jan, 28

Start by becoming aware of where your time and energy goes. Are you stuck in the details or out there seeing the bigger picture? Are you fixed in a routine or adaptable to things that come out of the blue? Whereas we can't change our fundamental personality, we can change our response to our life and we can certainly change our lives for the better.

EXERCISE ONE

1. This week read one book or newspaper than you've never picked up before.
2. Talk to a person you work with who you've never spoken to.
3. Listen to music you have never tried before and see how and why it makes you feel a certain way.

If you're stuck for where to begin, start by widening your world. Read new books, magazines and websites; listen to different music and differing politics; expose yourself to people you don't know; and use all of this to collect ideas, grow new passions and begin new projects. If you try to see every spare minute as a chance to grow, try something new or have an adventure, you'll have no time to be bored or fed up. This is dynamic living and it's within your grasp.

INSTANT NAUGHTY TASK

Do something different when you wake up tomorrow morning. Either get up half an hour earlier, or have breakfast at home if you always have it at work, watch breakfast TV if you usually listen to the radio, walk to work instead of taking the train. Change your pattern and see how it makes you feel.

STEP TWO

Better attitude, better work life

Making space for a newer, naughtier attitude is hard at work, especially when patterns and personalities seem set in stone, but it can be done and more easily than you think. First of all, using your new attitude, think about what's missing at work. Sometimes we assume we need a total 100 per cent change of career, when in fact all we need is a small step, and this changes everything. Take successful businesswoman/TV star/entrepreneur Oprah Winfrey; after years working as a journalist in television news she found herself demoted from the 6 o'clock news, to a daytime chat show and discovered, 'After all those years of feeling discontent, feeling I was in the wrong place, and in the wrong job, I found I was finally home.' And the rest is history.

The key to success and fulfilment in work is to change your attitude to work and think about the things that come naturally to you and that make you happy, even if that doesn't meet your definition of what work is and what your career should be. In other words, stop trying to fit into a circle when you're really more comfortable being a square or an oblong. To get ahead in life and get a better work attitude, play to your strengths. It seems obvious, but most people don't do it, especially at work, either because they're too vague about what they're good at or don't see their talents as talents, and therefore dismiss the idea that they can have a job that they love.

The good news is it's never too late to assess your passions, skills, desires and aptitude for certain careers. Once you've located them (see Desire section for more on this) the next challenge is to switch gears. Remember, as we said earlier, if you hold on to outdated beliefs for too long, sooner or later you'll come to believe them, so don't imagine you're too old or can't afford a pay cut to get what you want. Think of taking that side step via a different kind of job in the same field, or a different way of working via flexi time, or start again completely. To find out if you have the right work attitude, try the next exercise.

EXERCISE TWO

1. How did you choose your career/job?
2. Would you make the same decision if you had your time again?
3. What do you shine in and does your work life allow you to do this?
4. Which one thing could you change about yourself at work that would amaze your colleagues?

If your work life doesn't let you shine, then you have a choice apart from moaning: either look for your thrills outside of work, or change your attitude and persona in work by responding to people in a different way. Sometimes going from Miss Negative to Miss Positive can change the way your colleagues view you and your boss deals with you, and can even up your work profile. Likewise, speaking up, throwing out ideas and being proactive can help you feel more connected to what you do and more excited about it.

STEP THREE

Better attitude, better bounce-back

Studies show the condition of the mind influences our physical health (because the brain and the immune system communicate with each other). This explains why a positive mental attitude can help the body fight off disease and recover more quickly from illness. So consider your bounce-back ability not in terms of illness but in terms of life's setbacks! We've all been there, ready, willing and eager to start again only to have the first door slam in our face, or for everything to go wrong at the finishing line. How you respond when the worst happens says much about how good your attitude is about yourself, how much you trust yourself and how resilient you are. If you believe that you have the strength to go on and will come back from disaster no matter what, then you have fabulous bounce-back. If not, there are ways to boost your ability; for example:

To boost your belief in yourself:

- Think of all the times you thought the worst was going to happen and it did, and then you got over it. Reminding ourselves of what

90

we've withstood and overcome can help us to bounce back when smaller upsets happen and bigger ones loom.

- Get active. If you can't walk up stairs without getting out of breath, or throw ideas around in your head without feeling stressed, you'll never have faith in your physical and mental abilities and will always feel weaker in the presence of stronger people and in difficult situations.
- Let your attitude dictate your day for a change. You can do this both negatively – get up grumpy, snarl at everyone on your commute, find fault with everything, and be miserable and fed up – or do it positively, wake up and decide to be happy, smile on your commute and look for the best in everything that happens. Try both and be amazed at the impact you actually have on the state of your world.
- Get a support group; that is, get a group, not join one. We all need our safety nets and in most cases these are friends and families. Cultivate a strong support network that's willing to catch you when you fall hard but also willing to throw you back into the air once you're safe.

Joely, 32, came to the UK from America five years ago. She'd been head-hunted for a big producer job at a major UK television company and, uncharacteristically, had decided to grab the opportunity. After six weeks, despite selling up back home, ditching her boyfriend and moving her entire life thousands of miles, she was fired. 'Talk about hitting rock bottom at 100 mph', says Joely, 'never in my life had something gone so wrong so quickly. I called my mother and her response was that it served me right for getting above myself. I put the phone down and cried for two solid days.' During that time Joely's friends begged her to come home, her boyfriend said he'd take her back and the television company offered to pay her severance pay. Tempted as she was to slink home, Joely didn't, not because she was too embarrassed or because she felt ashamed, but because once she'd got over the shock of being fired, she realised that the job had been the catalyst for change in her life, not the reason for change. She realised that if she wanted her life to alter considerably she would have to find a way to bounce back – and bounce she did. She used her pay-off money to live on and spent three months researching a new web business venture; she signed up for a business course and now earns a very nice and tidy sum from a web design company. 'Has it been easy? Well, no, because there were lots of other things that went wrong along the way and lots of demons I had to face, but it's been worth it. I have my own business, a fabulous life here and the power of knowing I did it all myself, under my own steam, and I've never done that before.'

INSTANT NAUGHTY TASK
Think back to the last time something went wrong and you floundered. This time think about it and see how fast you can mentally turn the tables and bounce back.

EXERCISE THREE

To help yourself see your inner strengths, build what is known as a personal-fear pyramid. This is a list of your personal fears from one to ten, with one being your biggest fear and ten being your smallest anxiety.

For example:

1. I'm afraid of public speaking.
2. I'm afraid of confrontation.
3. I'm afraid of standing up to my partner.
4. I'm afraid of upsetting my mum.
5. I'm afraid of disappointing my family.
6. I'm afraid of making my boss angry.
7. I'm afraid of failing.
8. I'm afraid of questioning authority.
9. I'm afraid of saying 'I don't know' at work.
10. I'm afraid of telling my friends what I really think.

When you have your list, start at number ten and work your way through each fear. Your aim isn't to get to your biggest fear but to increase your belief in what you're actually capable of facing. Start slowly and face each fear gradually so that your fear lessens each time. For example, fear number ten (telling your friends what you think): start by giving your friends your opinion on, say, music, film or fashion, and then slowly build up to holding your ground on more confrontational things with them. This will help you to diminish the fear and increase your inner strength so that you aren't at the mercy of your fears and those people who are more assertive than you.

A word about attitude and coupledom

Can a relationship survive an attitude readjustment? Well, yes it can, especially if you have a supportive partner who's happy to see you change into a happier and braver being. Unfortunately change is also hard and threatening for someone who loves you because they imagine that in wanting more and seeking more, you are naturally going to move away from them and want someone else. Which is why it's essential that you keep loved ones in the loop. Tell them what you're doing and why.

This can be a journey together, but by being feistier, more courageous and upfront, as well as downright foolish just for the sake of it, it is a delicate balancing act within a relationship. Meaning, be aware of the effect your attitude is having around you. A loved one won't always come along for the ride if your pursuits seem one-sided and selfish or if you suddenly change your life plan without discussing it first. Likewise, if you change radically and swiftly, you have to expect that there will be an unsettled period within your relationship, so give your partner time to catch up.

Similarly, be aware that sometimes people who love you can be resentful if you're changing your life while they are still stuck in a rut, so be careful of being too OTT about the new and improved you. Breaking out of a comfort zone is difficult and stressful especially if you're not the one instigating the change, so be aware that new lives, like new businesses and new relationships don't happen overnight. They take time, planning, and shared goals and aims. Get your partner to see the bigger and wider picture by explaining all your steps, because if he can see the advantages of where you're heading and why, he'll be more than eager not only to support you but also to come along as well.

Freedom
MAKING YOUR ATTITUDE KICK

When I think of all the women I admire the most, the unifying aspect about them all is that they have wonderful attitudes about themselves, about life and about others. They have the kind of outlook you want to cling to in a storm, an easy way of turning a private disaster into something less devastating, and an ability to rally to your side as soon as life gets tough. They say the right thing, bolster you in the right way and are willing to give you that essential push when you're flagging and are about to give up. They have, as one person so rightfully said, 'contagious positive energy' and it is this that makes their attitudes kick.

What has all this got to do with you living a naughtier life? Well, to change direction, change opinions and change yourself, you also need that contagious positive energy, and this means you need to let your new attitude reach across your life a bit like a ripple effect, because an attitude that only changes you isn't one that kicks or lasts. To ensure your attitude keeps going and going and going you have to feed it everyday. It needs help, it needs positive reminders, and above all it needs lots and lots of experience to grow. To help keep the naughtier you kicking, ensure you do the following:

1. THINK INSPIRATION EVERY DAY

As in, be inspiring to others and keep yourself inspired. If you wake up every day and feel boredom sweeping over you, you're lacking in inspiration. Meaning, you haven't searched for inspiration for a while or are not allowing it into your life. Where do you find it? Well it's there in every person you meet, every book you read and each piece of music you hear, as long as you're open to it. This means being more externally aware than internally focused, which is a polite way of saying think less about yourself and more about what's going on around you.

On the whole, inspiration is anything that stimulates and encourages you. Anything that makes you want to leap off the couch and get going. To be inspiring let your attitude be infectious and instead of always being the bringer of doom and disaster be the person who says, 'go for it'.

2. RATE YOUR FUN QUOTA WEEKLY

Whether we're willing to admit it or not, we know if we're fun people or not. However, this is not an excuse to admonish yourself for not being a game person for others, but a wake-up call for when you're not living with attitude. This is because having fun doesn't mean fulfilling someone else's idea of a good time, but fulfilling your own. It's about making sure that 75 per cent of your life is entertaining and enjoyable, and if it's not, then working out why this isn't the case. Work, social life, downtime and relationships – these should be pleasurable for you, even in small doses. If any make your heart sink, you need to use your newfound attitude to change things, and fast.

3. BE WILLING TO MAKE A FOOL OF YOURSELF

Personally, this is the one I used to loathe the most, because, as a former good girl with a perfection streak, I didn't like to show the world I couldn't do things and have people laugh at my apparent uselessness (and thereby prove my secret theory about myself). However, by falling on my face regularly I learned a couple of things about myself. Firstly, that I am more resilient than I think, and that sometimes making a fool out of yourself is the best thing you can do to shake up your life because (1) it makes you human to the people who know and love you; and (2) it helps you to loosen up and take life less seriously. So, if you feel you're slipping back into your old ways, or feel you're holding on so tight because you're afraid you're going to fall or fail, leap in and make a fool out of yourself. Good opportunities are dancing, karaoke, public speaking and new sports.

4. BE WILLING TO SAY YOU DON'T KNOW WHEN YOU DON'T KNOW

Like your high-school teacher always said, you'll never learn anything if you're not willing to hold your hand up and admit you don't know the answer. Not the easiest thing to do in life, especially if you feel it will weaken your position and allow others to take advantage, but the fact is, saying 'I don't know' is an attitude eye opener. Why? Because it releases you from having to pretend all the time that you're in the know, allows others to see you as fallible (and there's real strength in that) and literally opens the door to more knowledge coming your way – something you can never get enough of!

5. START AGAIN WHENEVER YOU CAN

There's nothing more exhilarating than making a resolution that from tomorrow you and your life are going to be different. However, the reason most people blow their resolutions is that the second a resolution goes wrong they hop off the bus and consider themselves a failure. A new attitude is an amazing thing, and verve for a new life is even better, but in their early stages they can falter and are easily quashed by any type of derailment. So remember: whatever happens you can always start again from any point in your life. What's more it doesn't have to be marked by a specific day (1 January anyone?), a specific time (a forthcoming birthday) or even a specific event (job loss). Begin again; live again and reboot your attitude again any time you want or need to, because every day of your life is a chance for you to succeed.

One-month Attitude Planner

The aim of this month's planner is to take a step-by-step approach to changing your attitude not only to your life, but also towards other people and your inner self. This means looking at your behaviour and thinking about your choices and thoughts.

WEEK ONE

Monday   Think about who you tell the world you are through your behaviour, your body language, your tone and your verbal skills. What message are you sending out about yourself?

Tuesday   Attitude drives behaviour so if you find people always use you as a doormat or are aggressive to you, it's likely it's because you're telling them this is how you expect to be treated. Change your attitude about yourself and you'll change their response.

Wednesday   Really change your attitude for a day. Instead of being a 'yes' person or a negative person, spin your attitude on its head and see how people react to you. Are you surprised, frightened or amazed by how others treat you now?

Thursday   Consider what fuels your attitude. Are you angry or bitter or simply don't believe you deserve more? Where do these messages come from – your past, your parents or yourself?

Friday   List the last three times your attitude acted against you and how it made you feel. What could you have done differently to change the outcome?

Saturday   Spend less time today thinking about what you're doing wrong and focus on a new and improved attitude. Think less about what others think about you and more about what you think. Go out and for one night be externally (not internally) focused and see how that makes you feel.

Sunday   Cultivate a naughty attitude from now on. This is an attitude that dares you to risk, dares you to take chances and dares you to believe you can do what you set your mind to.

WEEK TWO

Monday   Recall all the things you're good at – whether it's personality traits, work skills, financial skills or even being able to make others laugh. Make up a list of these to challenge yourself with whenever you feel down on yourself.

Tuesday   Take a long hard look at your body language (or ask your best friend to do it). Think about how to walk into a room, sit, and how you respond when people talk to you or you talk to others. How could you improve your body language and put others at ease? Think posture – think about personal space (how near or far you get to a person) and think about how others make it work for themselves.

Wednesday   Think about the attitude of someone you admire and ask yourself what is it about them that impresses you or makes you wish you were more like them. Then compare it to your own attitude in a constructive way and think about how you could alter yours for the better.

Thursday   Come up with three goals that could radically change your attitude and your life for the better and put them into action. If you're stuck, think about being more daring, naughtier, and bolder about your decisions and your behaviour.

Friday   Avoid procrastination i.e. what might happen if you change, what might not happen and how you'll do it when you have more time/feel better/more enthusiasm. If you want to change, start now!

Saturday   This weekend have a holiday from yourself and for one day do all the things you'd never usually dare to do. It could be going into a fancy dress shop and trying on all the clothes, seeing three films in a row by yourself or even booking a holiday somewhere daring and unknown.

Sunday   Have a brainstorm with a group of close friends and work out ways you could put your new bolder attitude to good use. How could it improve your work life, your relationships and even the way you feel about yourself?

WEEK THREE

Monday   Work on changing your focus. Stop believing what others tell you about yourself and instead focus on what you know about yourself (in the positive) and what you know you're capable of. Every time you doubt yourself – refocus.

Tuesday   What have you always wanted to do/learn/try but have always been afraid of doing? Write down three things, collar your boldest friend and work your way through your list. When you feel nervous take a deep breath, and when you feel uncomfortable push through it – you'll be surprised at what you discover about yourself.

Wednesday Do something utterly frivolous and stupid today just for the sake of it. The idea is to stop feeling self-conscious and just do something for the sake of pure, unadulterated joy.

Thursday   Do something new – make a friend, change your daily routine and respond differently when something goes wrong. Challenge yourself to steer away from old habits and towards new ones.

Friday   Build your fear pyramid – the list of your personal fears from one to ten, with one being your biggest fear and ten being your smallest anxiety and work on knocking the blocks down.

Saturday   Let a positive attitude dictate your day for a change. Wake up and decide to be happy, smile, and look for the best in everything that happens. Then rate the impact it has on the state of your world.

Sunday	Build a support group that will encourage you to become the best you can from friends who are always there for you, colleagues who are not afraid to speak their mind, and mentors who inspire you. Your aim is to cultivate a strong support network that's willing to push you when you're stuck and catch you when you fall.

WEEK FOUR

Monday	Practise being inspiring all day by being the encouraging one to friends when they call, by acting positive at work in meetings and smiling all day when people speak to you and note the difference it makes to your mood and how others treat you.
Tuesday	If you're feeling that your new attitude hasn't yet taken off, make today your fresh start. You can start again any time you want and a new beginning can be yours with just one decision. Embrace what you want and take steps to go for it.
Wednesday	Do three brave things today that you'd never have done before. It could be something as simple as stand up for yourself to a friend or as big as book a round-the-world-trip.
Thursday	Practise being bold – that's bold in your choice of clothes for the day, bold in your choices to do with your life today and bold in how you speak and respond to others when you communicate.
Friday	De-clutter your life of all the things that bring you down. That's friends who make you feel bad, family members who are negative and the clothes and mementos that take you back to past and not into your new future.
Saturday	Make this the weekend of your dreams – go out and be the belle of the ball wherever you go. Take hours to get ready, pamper yourself, boost your esteem by surrounding yourself

with people who boost your confidence and have as much fun as you can fit into your day.

Sunday   Have a feel-good buying spree – go out and buy three things that inspire you to (1) feel good about the new you; (2) to keep moving forward in your life; and (3) make you feel happy. It can be an inspirational book, a picture, a CD or even a feel-good DVD.

Sexiness

Introduction

When it comes to sexiness, we are simply what we perceive ourselves to be. Meaning, if you believe your sexy years are behind you, or that you're not the sexy type and never have been, the chances are sexy living is but a distant dream. The good news is that like many things in life that feel impossible to grab hold of, sexy living can be yours and for less effort than you think, mainly because when I say 'get sexy' I am not just talking about orgasms, sexy underwear and a multitude of lovers – though these can be yours, too, if that's your dream – but simply your ability to live your life with passion, and find pleasure and satisfaction daily whether you're 25, 35 or 45 years old.

Contrary to popular belief, passion and sexiness don't have to disappear from your life once you reach a certain age and responsibilities creep in. Sexiness is not the domain of the young or the well endowed, you can be sexy at any age because you can be excited about life, have a sense of adventure and oozing sensuality at any age. Best of all, seeing that we all reach our sexual peak in our thirties, if you play your cards right your ability to flirt, look sexy and feel sexy can keep going up, too.

Of course, verve and passion are easy to throw on the back burner and forget about in the general ebb and flow of daily life, because who's got time to think sensual and be naughty when there are deadlines to meet and diets to go on? Which is why this section is all about getting sexy, feeling sexy and discovering how to live a sexy life.

Sexiness is a vital component of living a naughty-but-nice life, and essential if you're making over your self-esteem, because if you can't choose joy, pursue happiness and find pleasure in everything you do, whether it's stopping to smell a bunch of flowers, having sex or simply enjoying a laugh with a lover, then how are you ever going to feel satisfied with your life? Of course, injecting sexiness into your life can be tough, especially if (1) you don't know where to start; and (2) you feel faintly ridiculous about even considering it, but mark my words: learn to act sexy, make sexy decisions and you will lead a naughtier life.

Back when my own esteem was buried a few metres under my feet, I liked to feel I was too busy and serious for all that sexy nonsense. Flirting – no thanks, that was just too silly and manipulative for someone busy like me. Pleasure – no thanks, I was too busy delaying gratification for career power. Sexy clothes – no thanks, they were for other girls willing to take the easy route. I fooled myself that somehow I was living a more intellectual and smart life because I was willing to reject all that sexiness and look down my nose at having fun. I was being real – I'd tell friends I had no time for that silly frivolous stuff, such as orgasm talk, high heels and unadulterated passion, because it was only the fickle girls who spent their days looking good and seeking fun over the seriousness of life.

Of course, this was rubbish and a pretty good defence mechanism that allowed me the perfect get out from participating in life, because deep down inside I didn't really think these girls were silly, and I was envious of how they all had a bigger zest for life than me, and perplexed at how they just had so much more confidence and guts to go after what they wanted because, after all, it takes guts to be sexy. What's more, I realised it wasn't just about looks, because while some of these women were model material, most didn't seem to notice they were fat, thin, short, tall or unusual looking, and yet they still lived an amazingly sexy and open life.

> **'The sexiest woman I ever met was about two stone overweight, and short, yet, she had men eating out of her hand. I was shocked because for ages I just couldn't see what she had that I didn't. I realised afterwards that while I was sitting around feeling insecure and not good enough, she was busy charming the room, having fun and not worrying about what people like me thought. Now that's sexy!' Hannah, 28**

Later I realised it was all about self-worth – these girls had loads of it and I had none. These women valued themselves and so they didn't feel apologetic like I did about living a life that put their happiness first, because they knew that if they felt good, looked good and went for what they wanted then all the people around them would feel great, too.
So the first question to ask yourself is what makes you feel sexy and what doesn't? Write a list, conjure up a picture and/or do something that gives you pleasure right now. When I did a straw poll for this book the list of things that made women feel sexy and gave the instant feel-good factor went from the sublime (an appreciative look from a handsome stranger, a

foot massage, a unexpected kiss, a great dress and a deep belly-enhancing laugh) to the inspiring (crisp, clean and cool sheets, hot chocolate on a cold day, bare feet on summer grass, compliments from your best friend and losing yourself in your favourite song). It all makes for some very sexy living, and it can be yours.

Quiz

HOW SEXY ARE YOU?

Are you sexy, sassy or downright sad when it comes to passionate living?
Try this quiz to see how you score on the sexy scale and what you can do
to improve it.

1. **Which of these statements best reflect your view on being sexy?**
a. I used to be sexy when I was younger. (A)
b. I have my sexy moments. (C)
c. I've never been sexy and it doesn't bother me. (D)
d. I'm working towards being sexy. (B)

2. **How often do you flirt to get your way?**
a. Only when you feel confident and in the right company. (B)
b. You did when you were younger and could get away with it. (A)
c. Never – flirting is silly and manipulative. (D)
d. Only when you are drunk and lose my inhibitions. (C)

3. **Which of the following do you like the most about yourself?**
a. Your body – 'I work hard to stay in shape.' (A)
b. Your intellect – 'It's never let me down.' (B)
c. Your face – 'I know I'm pretty.' (C)
d. None of the above. (D)

4. Your sex appeal would be most improved by:

a. A sexier body, preferably thinner. (C)

b. Plastic surgery. (A)

c. More sex, more lovers, and more male attention. (B)

d. A change in your attitude about what being sexy equals. (D)

5. You admire sexy women for their …

a. You don't admire women for being sexy. (D)

b. Amazing bodies. (C)

c. Guts and courage to live the way they want. (B)

d. Youthful looks and wardrobes. (A)

6. Sexy is …

a. Someone else. (D)

b. Young and fresh. (A)

c. A state of mind. (B)

d. Hard work. (C)

7. What gives you the highest pleasure quota in life?

a. Sex and looking good. (A)

b. Your friends and family. (B)

c. Food and/or drink. (C)

d. Work and/or your home. (D)

8. To have more pleasure and passion in your life you would need …

a. To change your attitude totally. (D)

b. To turn back the clock. (A)

c. To have more guts to go after what you want. (B)

d. More time. (C)

Results

Add up all the answers you gave that were followed by (A) and then those followed by (B), and so on. Then see which score was the highest. If you scored highest on the (A) answers that makes you Past Sexy, see below. If you scored highest on the (B) answers that makes you Half-sexy, and so on.

PAST SEXY (mostly As)

Your beliefs about being sexy and living a sexier life are locked into the idea that sexy is the domain only of the young and nubile. Whether this is something you feel is proved to you over and over or an indication that you're no longer happy with your looks and life, only you can say.

However, bear in mind that we never see things as they are; we see things as we are. Meaning, if you feel that sexiness has gone out of your life it's because you no longer feel sexy about yourself. If you want to lead a life with more pleasure you need to view yourself and your choices in a more passionate way. Sexiness and verve can be yours at any age if you go after them, nurture them and make up your mind to live that way. Read on to find out how.

HALF-SEXY (mostly Bs)

You have the desire to be sexier and live a sexier life, but your confidence is lagging and so you often give up just before you get there. Try also to see that sexy is something that goes beyond the realms of sex and relationships. It's about feeling you're glorious, that you can have a life that's full of vitality and joy, and that you have power and energy in everything you do. In a nutshell, sexiness should be your essence and something that's with you all the time, not just when you're out and about having a good time dressed up to the nines. Get it right and you'll feel it even when you're lounging about without make-up in a grubby pair of track-pants.

WANNABE SEXY (mostly Cs)

There's a part of you desperate to be sexy, but as the word seems so alien to you you're unsure of where to start and where to go with it. Maybe it's the actual word 'sexy' that is your stumbling block. If so, try to aim for sexiness outside the realms of sex and being what society calls sexy. It doesn't have to mean high heels, flirty behaviour and orgasms galore. Living a sexy life is simply about living the life you want: making choices that are passionate and choosing the things that give you true pleasure. What's more, doing it your own way is what's really sexy in life – look around you and you'll see that it's true.

NEGATIVE SEXY (mostly Ds)

It's likely that you are condemning of sexy women and being sexy in general simply because you feel it's beneath you to try to fit a stereotype of what it means to be a sexy woman. If so, you need to re-evaluate what you mean by 'sexy' because sexy means passion and verve. It means having the guts to be yourself, feeling good about who you are and positive about being a woman and the choices you make. It's also about feeling attractive and giving yourself worth, not about being someone you're not. Bearing all that in mind, isn't it time to get sexy?

Sexiness
FACING THE FACTS

If you saw yourself enter a room, what would you think about yourself? There goes a girl who's happy, sexy and confident? Or would you notice an embarrassed glance, sloped shoulders and hesitant attitude? Would you assume this person was leading a passionate life, full of pleasure, or worrying herself into the ground about what others thought of her clothes, hair and make-up? Now picture the sexiest woman you know and consider what you think about her as she enters a room. What do you notice first about her, how does she make you feel (outside of a little insecure) and how does she work the room and what does her expression say, compared to yours?

It's likely her face says, 'I'm having a great time', because I guarantee you she is. Not just in a room but in her life as a whole, and not just because she looks good. As a woman who used to be Queen of Low Self-esteem, I used to loathe sexy women like that, not just because they were capable of getting admiring glances from everyone in a room but also because when you actually met them they were so nice. No secretive bitching in a corner for them and no self-deprecating humour that made you feel awkward, these women were simply generous to a fault and good fun with it. It's a hard pill to swallow when you really want them to fulfil the stereotype of a vain and egotistic woman, but sexy women were, I realised, amazing fun to be around.

I now realise that sexy women are like that simply because they don't waste all their time and energy worrying about all the things that seem so important when you're someone who is constantly down on yourself. Worries such as what others will think and say about you; worries about your reflection so that it stops you from going out; and worries about not being all the things you want to be, to the point that it stops you from actually going after it, are debilitating. If all that sounds familiar, it's time to stop thinking about all the reasons why you're not sexy and start acting sexy! Here's how:

STEP ONE

WARNING – pleasure-starved life ahead!

Seek out pleasure – it's the number-one tip for any wannabe sex bomb, because if you know what makes you happy and makes you feel good, you know how to be sexy. So ask yourself: do you take your pleasures seriously or are they just the small treat at the end of a long, hard and boring day? Are they the distant gifts that make you work harder, stay at work longer and deny yourself more and more and more? If so, you need what's known as a pleasure overhaul, because pleasure is something that should be on your mind and in your life every day, especially if you want to live a sexier, and naughtier, life. And yes, it is possible to have fun every day if you learn to take pleasure in everything you do, not just your free time, but also your work time, your domestic time and even your commuting time.

Of course, some pleasures will always have a higher score than others in your life – feeling desired by someone you love, having mind-blowing sex, laughing so hard you cry and even savouring a long, cold drink on a hot day will, for some, rate pretty sky-high on the pleasure scale. But alongside this you also need to work at finding pleasure in yourself and all the things you do outside of the obvious joys, so that you feel buoyed up with confidence and esteem for most of your time.

If you're a glass half-empty kind of girl who's scoffing at all of this and just can't believe turning into Pollyanna will help, well, it won't if it goes against your true nature (more on that below), but before you dismiss the glass half-empty theory you need to consider that your ability to be sexy, feel good about yourself and find pleasure comes from how you view your whole life, not just one aspect of your life – so what have you got to lose by trying things a different way for a change. The fact is that if you compartmentalise your sexiness and naughtiness into, say, your looks, or your sex life, or your holidays and weekends, then all you're doing is telling yourself that you can't be happy all the time – and you can.

Sexiness is a state of mind that will help you reap pleasure every day if you let it. Be someone who finds delight in a sunny day, enjoyment in a flirty exchange with a stranger, or bliss within a book or a song, and you're actually being someone who is opening herself to all the different passions there are in life. If you can't do this and you feel your life is currently pleasure-starved (and you'll know it is if you dread getting up every day, live for your nights and generally see no light at the end of the tunnel), then it's time to look at what your beliefs are when it comes to pleasure, passion and sexiness, and then to turn things around.

The answers to Exercise One should give you clear ideas about what beliefs you're holding when it comes to why you're living a pleasure-starved life. The main way to

116

EXERCISE ONE

1. Our attitudes about pleasure and sexiness have a lot to do with our backgrounds, so ask yourself how pleasure and passion were viewed in your house.
   a. Were you encouraged to hold it in and delay gratification?
   b. Was happiness and pleasure seen as something positive?
   c. Were you told that real life is not about fun but hard work?
2. Does the way you live your life now represent the view from your childhood or is it radically different?
3. If you have a radically different view that's more negative, what key moments from your adult life have created your outlook and beliefs about your appeal and how you live your life?
4. What's your greatest pleasure and how often do you allow yourself to enjoy it?

improve your pleasure quota is to think consciously about what brings you happiness and joy. What makes you happy, feel thrilled, and literally jumping for joy? When do you most feel confident and happy about yourself?

Now think about how often you allow yourself to feel pleasure. Is it daily? Is it monthly? Or only when others give you permission? In order to get sexy you need to allow yourself to have fun all the time, because this is the essence of sexiness. Steps to boosting your pleasure are simple. Start by writing a list of all the things that give you pleasure, no matter how small or how big. Then next to them give them a rating out of ten.

For example:

- Making someone laugh 10/10
- Reading a great book 10/10
- Doing something for someone 10/10
- Receiving compliments 5/10
- Looking in the mirror and feeling good 8/10
- Having someone look at me appreciatively 8/1
- Strawberry ice cream 4/10
- Laughing until I cry 10/10
- Listening to music 6/10
- Good sex 7/10
- Magazines 5/10
- People-watching 5/10
- Talking with friends 7/10
- Staying in when it's cold 5/10
- The smell of coffee 5/10
- The smell of freshly mown grass 5/10
- Being wrapped up in bed when it's raining outside 8/10

Anything that rates above 7/10 is something you should be doing every day, and if you're not, ask yourself why? You're allowed to be happy and you're allowed to seek out pleasure in everything you do – work, play and home life. If your pleasures are limited to one area, work out how you could bring the same attitude you save, say, for your social life into your work life and even your daily life. Remember it's more than possible to love what you do and even enjoy work (even if you would rather be somewhere else entirely) and it's more than possible to let pleasure seep through your day from start to finish if you start to appreciate what you're doing and how you're living. Check your list for ideas.

STEP TWO

Get sexy

Also known as: start to think, act and behave in a sexy way. Nothing makes you sexier faster than being more daring in life, which often means shaking yourself out of your current state by changing something about the way you portray yourself to others. This is not about changing your clothes (more on that in Style) but about changing your behaviour, as sometimes even a simple change in your reactions can have an astounding effect on how you view yourself and how others treat you.

For example, take Zoe, 26: for a week she decided to change the way she talked about herself. 'As an expert in the art of self-flagellation I realised after a day that putting myself down all the time not only destroyed my confidence but also my mood. In making myself be positive about myself I felt totally different and more confident. Better still, people treated me differently and I realised that by being negative about myself all the time all I was doing was teaching other people how to view me.'

So if, like Zoe, you're someone who's always pointing out your flaws, saying you're fat/unsexy/horrible and showing people you're not the sexy type, then that's how they'll see you. Be aware that you may not do it overtly like Zoe, and it may show itself in one of the following ways:

I. NEGATIVE BODY LANGUAGE

This is when your posture shows you are defeated before you've even said or done anything. Bad posture is shown by the way you hold your head and shoulders, the way you walk and the way you stand, and the way you maintain (or refuse to maintain) eye contact when speaking.

Solution: Hold your head up (imagine a piece of string pulling you up from the centre of your skull) and pull your stomach in, this immediately causes your whole body to pull upwards and improves your posture.

2. NEVER FEELING COMPETENT

This is the feeling that you're going to make a fool of yourself, embarrass yourself or do something wrong, and is an indication that you simply don't feel you're good enough.

Solution: Say to yourself, 'So what!' if you do something wrong, 'it's not the end of the world' and put your fears into perspective.

3. FEARFULNESS

You're afraid to meet new people and enter new situations and so you stay in your comfort zone. Sadly, sexy women do the opposite – they push beyond what they're comfortable with and confront change head on.

Solution: Confront your fears (see the personal-fear pyramid in the Attitude section).

4. PERFECTIONISM

This is the need always to look perfect and appear perfect to others and is bad news in the sexy stakes, because if sexy women are one thing it's imperfect. They aren't afraid to show their flaws, appear dishevelled and even say and do the wrong thing, because they know it doesn't matter.

Solution: Work out what you're getting from being a perfectionist – what does it give you an excuse to avoid?

5. OVER-IDENTIFICATION WITH THE VALUES OF OTHERS

This is where you believe everyone else's opinion is more valid than your own and so let others lead your life.

Solution: To change this take an inventory of your life and ask yourself what you can do today that's different and will change the way you feel about your life.

EXERCISE TWO

What are you telling the world about yourself?

1. What does your voice and dress sense say about you? Do they project confidence, fear, shyness or authority?
2. What changes could you make to your voice and appearance that would make you feel sexier and more confident?
3. How do you respond to sexy women? What do you wish you had that they have (apart from looks)?

To change your attitude to your life try one of the following in a positive way and note how it makes you feel in terms of your sexiness and vitality:

- Behave in a different way when you meet a friend for a drink.
- Respond in a different manner when asked to do something you don't want to do.
- Answer in a different way when you pick up the phone.
- Buy something you like but usually feel afraid of buying.
- Speak out when you would usually stay quiet.
- Walk with your head held high when you cross a room or bar.
- Flirt with someone for fun in a shop.
- Be understanding, not annoyed, when someone makes a mistake.
- Smile when someone looks at you.
- Talk to a stranger on your way home.

INSTANT NAUGHTY TASK
Act sexy tonight (see the above list for ideas) and see where it leads you.

STEP THREE

Rethink your views on sexiness

To ignite your sexiness it's important to know what equals sexy in your book. If your idea of a sexy woman is a supermodel with legs that reach up to the sky, or a glamour model with larger than average breasts, then sexiness for you, like many people, is entrenched in the physical. Whereas sexiness is about more than this; in order to see yourself as sexy you first need to first make peace with your looks. Easier said than done, of course, especially if you have a love–hate relationship with your body and can't see its good points, thanks to all your perceived bad points.

I'm not saying your bad points don't exist or that you should ignore them, but I'm just pointing out that you have to see worth in your body no matter what size or shape you are. If you don't like your body then you have a choice: work on changing it via diet and exercise, or work on emphasising your strong bits and boosting your weak bits, because in order to feel good you can't separate your body from your mind. To help create a more positive body image:

1. **Stop comparing yourself to others. This is a hard one because we all evaluate ourselves in relation to others. However, do so all the time and all that will happen is you'll either feel smug or crushed by what you see.**
2. **Stop harping back to the good old days when you looked amazing, or stop dreaming about a future day when you'll look amazing.**
3. **Focus on the present and see what's great about you right now. What could be tweaked and what could be tidied up (see Style for more on**

this)? What could you emphasise and what could you hide?

4. Don't have an all-or-nothing attitude; that is, 'I can't be sexy until I'm a size 10', or 'I can't be sexy because I don't have big breasts or long legs'. Sexy takes all sorts, look around you for evidence of this.

5. Don't personalise everything; that is, I didn't get asked out because I'm ugly and un-sexy! I didn't get that job because they think I am dull. Think rationally about yourself.

Take Kate, 32, who says, 'When I was 20 years old I wish I'd known what I know now that I don't have to be thin and pretty to be valuable and feel good. Now I am older I'm definitely sexier, because I no longer rely on the affirmation of others to feel good about myself. I know what suits me and what doesn't and I know what gives me confidence and what doesn't and I use that to drive my life and decisions, not my weight or my bra size. It's taken me years to get here but I'm definitely sexy now.' As Kate says, using other people's standards to measure your worth is a losing

EXERCISE THREE

1. Stand naked before a full-length mirror, and look at your face and body.
2. Look closely at the body parts you don't like and notice how they make you feel.
3. What parts of your body make you feel comfortable; what parts do you feel like hiding?
4. Get used to seeing yourself naked like this at least once a day – this desensitises you to the shock of being naked and helps you to start seeing yourself as someone with good and not-so-good parts.

battle. Meaning, you need to look within for validation, and this means accepting your physical self and loving your body for what it is now, not what it could be or what you could change about it. It's not an easy thing to do but it can be done, and it all starts by learning to see and appreciate your body for what it is. Remember: there is no perfect equation for sexiness – no perfection you have to aim for, and no ideal – just work on being appealing to yourself. Don't apologise for who you are in your head or in life. Get body-confident and your mind will follow.

It's important not to be ashamed of praising your good points in the parts of you that you like. We're all guilty of magnifying our faults and overlooking the parts of us that make us unique and sexy. If you're someone who doesn't want to admit to them, either because you're afraid of being vain, or assume it's egotistical, then you need to change your mindset, and fast. Celebrating your body has nothing to do with conceit; it's about acknowledging you have much to offer and feeling proud of who you are right now. Remember: when you believe you are sexy, and are willing to say you are sexy, you'll exude sexiness.

INSTANT NAUGHTY TASK
Do three things today that boost your body-confidence: pamper yourself, get active and buy something sexy.

STEP FOUR

Build a sexy outlook

If none of this sexy advice has worked on you so far, you need to ask yourself what you're hoping for in the make-me-sexy stakes: plastic surgery, hypnotism or maybe a magic answer to help you feel instantly good? Well, I hate to tell you this but rebuilding your self-esteem is hard work, especially when you've spent years sitting comfortably in one mode of thinking. However, one facet that can help you live a naughtier and sexier life is to take a long, hard look at your outlook on sexiness.

For example, are you like Hannah, 24, who says 'I only feel sexy when I have a boyfriend because then I know I am attractive'! Or like Dawn, 26, who believes she will be sexy when she gets 'breast implants, a nose job and loses two stone'. Or are you still battling with the idea that sexy is something you're not meant to be, either because of past messages from loved ones or beliefs you've built up?

If so, it's worth asking yourself what does a sexier life mean to you?

- Is it the desire to be someone else?
- Is it to live a life more fully?
- Is it about being desired by others or knowing you're a desirable person?

If you're stuck, think about who you consider to have a sexy life, and why? What's that certain something that your favourite sexy women have that you feel you don't? Think about their looks and their confidence, their charisma and the guts they have to go after what they want in life. To help yourself get a sexier outlook:

1. BROADEN YOUR HORIZONS

You're always going to feel stuck in a dull and drab life if you see the same people all the time, do the same things and have the same conversations over and over with friends. Nothing's sexier than a person who's well travelled, well read and knowledgeable about a wide range of subjects. How do you know you're not interested in deep-water diving if you've never given it a go? Or how do you know living abroad is not for you if you haven't tried to learn a new language. Be like Alison, 27, who, after ten years of being in a couple, found herself single and in a serious rut where she was doing the same thing day in and day out and socialising with the same friends over and over. In two years she changed all that and went from someone who wouldn't say boo to a goose to a girl who willingly skydived off a mountain in South Africa, learned to speak Italian at night school, started her own business out of her bedroom and cut her gorgeous long hair into an impish bob. She's definitely sexy and she's definitely hot.

2. TRY NEW THINGS

Of course you don't have to go skydiving to be sexy or even do anything radical like cut off your hair but you do have to be willing to try new things. Sexy and naughty lives thrive on excitement and adventure,

EXERCISE FOUR

For one day:

1. Change one thing about your look: wear a different colour, a skirt instead of jeans, heels instead of trainers, or something fitted if you usually go baggy.
2. Change one thing about your social life: suggest to friends you go somewhere you've never been before or go to a bar alone and talk to someone for half an hour.
3. Change one thing about your behaviour at work: be positive and upbeat about everything you're given to do.

Then note:

1. How you feel about your confidence at the end of the day.
2. How people responded to you both positively and negatively.
3. How you felt about living differently.

because this is the ideal way to boost confidence and bolster self-belief. This is mainly because once you know you can survive change, and risk the misery of disappointment, nothing ever feels so scary again.

So make a list of all the new things you'd like to try but haven't yet had the guts to do. It can be anything from learning to drive, or swim, or ice-skate, or sing. It could be trying a new type of food – perhaps something spicy if you're usually a plain eater, or something exotic if you're currently a meat-and-two-vegetables type of girl. If you're single, date lots of different people, because you can never be sure who your type is! If you're coupled up, surprise your partner in bed and out by showing him that there's more to you yet. Be bold, be decisive, and live sexily.

3. DO THINGS WITH GUSTO

Finally, learn to do things with gusto and verve – half-hearted attempts to try new things or even do the things you do all the time, aren't enjoyable and are rarely successful, so practise doing things with passion. If in doubt as to how to do this, just take a deep breath, imagine a fantastic outcome, stop worrying and jump in. Sink or swim, doing something with passion means you'll enjoy yourself, sex up your life and generally have a far better time than you could ever have imagined.

INSTANT NAUGHTY TASK
Make one of the above changes something you do once a week.

Sexiness rehab
HOW TO BE SEXIER

Hopefully by now you should be well on the way to having a sexier outlook and attitude, so to cement your status as a 'nearly-there sex bomb' it's time to talk about sex! Sex, a sexier life and self-esteem go hand in hand (as do sex and a naughtier life, for that matter) – because, let's face, it if you don't feel good about yourself and your body, the chances of feeling good in bed, having a good time in bed, and even liking sex are pretty limited. The good news is that it's never too late to have a sexual awakening and literally change your views about what equals good sex, and what you feel about sex.

Part of the problem with sex is that when we start our sex lives we are all basically insecure creatures desperate not to do the wrong thing. This makes us vulnerable to others who seem to know what they're doing and media depictions of what equals hot sex. On top of this we are bombarded with information and advice on what makes a good lover, what makes us sexy and what doesn't, to the point that it's easy to get intimidated or stuck in a sexual rut for life.

If you feel you fail miserably in bed and when you look in the mirror, then rest assured there's hope – not only can you turn your sexual status around but you can also add spark to your current sex drive. All you have to do is understand what it is you want from sex (besides orgasms) and how you feel about sex. These two things will improve your sex life and help you to feel sexier in and out of bed. The last point is important because it's rare to find a woman who's sexy in bed, who isn't also sexy out of it; meaning, get it right in the bedroom and you'll be able to bring your newfound sexiness into other areas of your life as well. Alongside this, discovering what makes you tick sexually, and what's what with sex in general, can help you feel less insecure about having sex, so that when things inevitably get embarrassing or awkward you won't let it crush your self-esteem and self-worth.

STEP ONE

Get naked and love it

The most testing thing most women face when it comes to enjoying sex and feeling sexy is body shame. Being the girl who used to be most likely to cover up on the beach, I know first hand that unless you spent your childhood days wandering bare then you're unlikely to feel fabulous in the nude. But the naked truth is this: although most of us are bummed about how we look without clothes, you have to feel good about yourself naked if you want to enjoy sex and feel sexy. Why? Well it's impossible to relax enough to have an orgasm if you're too worried about your breasts drooping or your cellulite showing.

One way to feel better about your body is to simply get used to being naked and seeing yourself naked. The fact is the more you get used to what being naked feels like, the more comfortable you'll be with your body.

'The first time I stood in front of a mirror naked I couldn't look at myself. I mean I really couldn't. I had to look through my fingers and stand there for about 40 seconds before I could open my eyes properly and see my body. How ridiculous is that? No wonder I was so hung up in bed.' Sam, 28

You may not realise it but for many of us our clothes are a security blanket and so we rarely get naked for more than about ten minutes a day. Take Sara, 28, who admits, 'until very recently I never looked at my body naked. I'd take all my clothes off and hop in the shower as quickly as I could. Then jump out and wrap a towel round me. I'd get dressed and only then look in the mirror. When I was home alone I'd never even think to strip off and walk from one room to the next – I just wasn't someone who was the naked type. Then I started seeing a new man and he is Mr Naked – he thinks nothing of sitting down to breakfast in the nude or strolling from one room to the next. He's so calm and matter-of-fact about it that he's helped me feel less self-conscious about my own nakedness, and a by-product of this is it's made me feel less self-conscious about my body. I feel more comfortable about my lumpy bits and far less critical about myself as a whole.'

Thankfully, you don't have to wait to meet your own Mr Naked to get to grips with your nakedness but be aware when you strip off that at first you're bound to feel:

- Vulnerable – this is completely normal and natural because you're literally laying yourself bare to yourself and the world, but the feeling will pass the more you do it.

- Silly – again this is normal because it does feel foolish to walk about with nothing on, even if you're all alone and the curtains are drawn, but get naked every day and eventually confidence will win out over self-consciousness.
- At odds with your body – this is because we all imagine we know what we look like but often we don't. However, don't panic, because looking down at your naked body is always hugely unflattering, as the angle makes you appear out of proportion. It's always best to view yourself straight on in a mirror and make sure you look at yourself as a whole and for at least two minutes, to let the whole picture sink in properly.

EXERCISE ONE

1. Are you self-conscious about your naked body? If so, is it the way you were brought up, or is it because you currently don't like your body? Or do you have unrealistic ideals about body perfection and/or your weight?
2. Is your response to your body at odds with the reaction of your lover or past lovers?

The aim of the above exercise is to make you aware that maybe you're more comfortable criticising your body than being comfortable with it. Growing up and hearing negative comments can make anyone paranoid about how they are perceived, but it's crucial to curb these thoughts, because if you don't they will have a huge impact on your sex life, your ability to wear the sexiness mantle, and your self-worth.

To curb the critic within:

- Every time you catch yourself criticising your body, replace every negative with a balancing positive; for example, my thighs are disgusting but my legs are long; my breasts are too big but I have a good cleavage; my eyes are too close but they're a great colour. If you do this every single time you'll eventually start doing it automatically and, remember, the brain believes what we tell it, so be nice to yourself.
- Accept compliments. This is a huge one, because if you can't bring yourself to believe the nice things that are said to you, what you are basically saying is that everyone is lying to you, and why would they do that? Think about the compliment, savour it and then remind yourself of it when you feel down.
- Do something positive. If you think you're too flabby or too fat, don't just fall into a downward spiral where you beat yourself up all the time. Do something about it: join a gym, lose weight or dress more effectively (see Style for more on this).
- Spoil yourself. Women with low body confidence tend not to pamper themselves because they feel they don't deserve it. This is rubbish. Look after your body with pampering products and you'll start to appreciate how it feels and how good it can really look.

INSTANT NAUGHTY TASK
Do something to make yourself feel body-confident today. What would do it for you? A massage, new underwear, some beauty pampering? Indulge yourself and enjoy!

STEP TWO

Go on a charm and flirting offensive

If you are someone who hates the idea of flirting because you assume it's manipulative and somewhat stupid, it's time to change your view, because flirting is all about charm and charisma, and without these things you can never truly be sexy. Charming people are true naughty-but-nice people because they know how to work a room, how to be ballsy and how to use their best skills to win people over without being manipulative. They are the queens of body language and verbal skills and adept at reading others so much so that if you know someone like this it's likely you're drawn to them because they have the ability to bring out the very best in you.

If you're not a flirting natural, you need first to focus on what's known as your interpersonal skills. This refers to the way you communicate with others both at work and in social situations. Someone with good inter-personal skills will know how to read a stranger and get the best out of them using very little information. If this doesn't come naturally to you, you need to pay more attention to the non-verbal signals people give you, for example:

I. BODY LANGUAGE

Is their body backing away from you as you approach, or does it look open and welcoming to you? When you look someone in the eye, do they make eye contact, and does their smile reach their eyes (this determines a real smile)? Are they looking at you as you speak or over your shoulder?

EXERCISE TWO

To help yourself the next time you're out with friends or in a work meeting see if you can read people's body language when you speak to them.

1. Say something controversial, and watch how people respond via their body language and vocal tone.
2. Say something complimentary or remind people of a time when they did well, and note the difference in their body language and attitude.
3. Think about how you respond to people in stressful situations – what can you change about the messages you send out?
4. How do changes in your body language and tone affect the people around you?

2. TONE AND ATTITUDE

You can hear a lot about what someone says from their tone of voice – is it even and paced out or nervous and jumpy? Are their words aggressive or soothing? Does their tone appear different from their words?

The next thing you need to do is boost your flirting skills so that you can charm anyone, anytime. The first thing you need to bear in mind is that flirting takes hard work and time to get right, so don't expect to become confident in it overnight. Secondly, whereas there are tried-and-tested flirting tips it's always best to do it your way; that is, the way that works for you. Lastly, flirt appropriately, and be aware that flirting if used in the wrong way can get you into a whole heap of problems. Here's how to perfect the art.

3. TAKE RISKS

Be prepared to take risks, as in taking social risks to boost your flirting skills. If you're someone who usually wouldn't say boo to a goose, or waits to be invited or talked to at a party, step up and make the first move. Initiate conversations, introduce yourself to people you don't know, chat up people you like the look of, and take a deep breath, walk into a room alone, smile and see what happens. To begin with, flirt with anyone and everyone, as this helps you to hone your skills, and gets you used to flirting with the opposite sex. See what techniques (see below) you feel comfortable with, what you can't quite handle and what you need to work on. And don't take it too seriously – flirting is fun, so lighten up when you do it.

> **'I'm a terrible flirt and I know it. I flirt with men I fancy, I flirt with female friends to make them feel good and I flirt to get more coffee in my local café. It's not manipulative – it's about being charming, being friendly and just making people feel good because you can.' Lucy, 28**

4. USE YOUR EYES

'I love his/her eyes' is a common refrain from lovers, and it's not surprising when you think your eyes are probably your most important flirting tools. The visual impact aside, our eyes are powerful transmitters of social signals. Think of how rarely you stare at someone in the eyes and how inappropriate it is to do so (people read long stares as threatening or odd), which is why when you're flirting your initial eye contact lasts just a few seconds. When you're trying to attract someone, the ideal way to signal your interest is by holding your target's gaze for more than one second. If his eye contact is returned, the chances are that he may be interested. If this happens, look away, and within a second return your gaze, if he's still looking, he's interested, so go over and speak to him. All you have to do is say 'hello'.

However, don't get too focused on eye contact once you move beyond this initial attraction because once a conversation begins, it is normal for the person who is speaking to look away more than the person who is listening. Stare too intently and/or read too much into what he's doing with his eyes and you'll make the object of your flirt uncomfortable.

5. HAVE A CONVERSATION

Also known as avoid 'chat-up lines' because your opening line is really not very important; it's what you say after you say hello that counts. So think about initiating a conversation, rather than impressing someone with a one-liner. You don't have to be witty, smart or clever, just friendly, so think of what you're trying to get across, what you want to find out and above all about having a good time for the time you're together.

To do this, act interested and be interesting. Ask questions, listen to answers and don't hog the conversation. The essence of a good flirt is something known as reciprocal disclosure, whereby you offer something personal and they return with something personal, as this is the perfect way to escalate the level of intimacy without revealing too much.

6. USE YOUR BODY

Touching is a powerful flirting tool, but be careful of how you use it. Tactile gestures can be used to express agreement, sympathy, or simply to convey affection. The first rule, however, is to avoid giving misleading signals with over-familiar touches – the face, intimate areas like the chest and the bottom and tops of legs are out of bounds, as they put people off or just scream sex, instead of sexy. But a gentle touch on the arm or the hand, nodding and not crossing your arms are all registered as reassuring and warm, and will enhance someone's feelings towards you and should prompt some reciprocal increase in intimacy such as more smiling, moving closer to you or mirroring your body language.

7. ZAP SELF-CONSCIOUSNESS

People assume others think they are boring when they are actually bored with themselves, so give your charisma a boost by reminding yourself of all the ways you sparkle. Make a list if you have to, but remind yourself what you've got going for you and then refuse to feel awkward. It can help to remind yourself that you've got to be in it to win it. Meaning, you'll never feel brave and self-assured if you hide in the shadows and wait to be spoken to. The benefits of learning to flirt and getting good at it are also huge in terms of your self-esteem and self-worth. Get it right and you'll never be afraid to enter a room/party/meeting alone again. You'll feel more relaxed when someone flirts with you and completely empowered by the effect your smile, your glance and even your words can have on someone you meet, and that, in a nutshell, is pure sexiness!

INSTANT NAUGHTY TASK
Flirt with someone on your way to work, at work and on your way home, and each time give yourself a rating out of ten for it.

STEP THREE

Sex up your sex life

If you've ever sat in a bar and heard tales of how your friends have had ten heart-stopping orgasms in a row, and are just plain exhausted because their sex life is so energetic and full on, you have my sympathy. As an ex-sex columnist I always noticed how women fell into two camps whenever the topic of sex came up: the 'I'm-having-fabulous-sex' group and the 'I'm sick-with-envy-about-your-sex-life' group. The former group all walked around looking like sex goddesses while the other group tended to look as if they wanted the ground to open up and swallow them. The funny thing was, I also noticed when it came to who was having hot sex, looks had very little to do with it, as the women were as varied a bunch as you could get, but the only thing that unified them was sexual confidence – they had it and the other women didn't.

So what makes for good sexual confidence? Well, contrary to popular belief it's not a body to die for or a good lover, but simply a good attitude to sex. The fact of the matter is that sex doesn't work for thousands of women but, because most don't know what to do about it, they keep this fact hidden and fake it for life. The reality is, no one is born being good at sex; like any skill it's something we all have to learn, which means wherever you are now on the sexual scale it's more than possible to sex up your life, feel more sexual confidence and exude the allure of a sex goddess. Here's how:

1. DO YOUR SEX HOMEWORK

If you don't know what does it for you in the orgasm stakes or what his extra bits do for him, or even what it takes to get you feeling sexy in the first place (clothes, music, a touch, and so on) you're fighting a losing a battle. Luckily, this is easily solved by doing some basic anatomy field-work, which means: think about what turns you on, how you feel in certain clothes, and what has to be said to you to make you feel sexy.

Stuck for what to do in bed? Then get some ideas by educating yourself with books, films and sex books. Above all make sex a priority in your life, not something that just happens between the sheets late at night. This means, feel sexy, and get sexy by sexing up your image (see Style) and your environment, and allow yourself to squeeze every drop of excitement out of sexy living.

2. TALK ABOUT SEX

Do you find sex too embarrassing to talk about? Are you worried your boyfriend can't handle criticism or the idea that maybe you're not satisfied? Well, you may be surprised at his reaction. In a recent sex survey 95 per cent of men said they wanted to know if their girlfriends were actually enjoying sex because they never let on. So have a tactful and constructive discussion about what turns you on and what he likes. If words fail you then try being loud about your appreciation. Moan, yell, and wriggle about when he does something right and then try directing him by moving his hands to where you want him to be. On top of this, get used to talking about sex in general. Discuss it with your girlfriends, discuss it out of bed, and make it a topic that's present in your life so that it becomes part of who you are.

3. FAKE IT UNTIL YOU MAKE IT

Sometimes the best way to get sexy fast is to literally fake sexiness to feel it. Dress sexy (it doesn't have to be the stereotype of sexy, but your version), think sexy – try erotica books, sexy pictures – and create a sexy mindset about yourself. Emphasise your best bits, work on your charisma (see the section above) and when you're having sex if you feel self-consciousness creeping in, switch off, fake enthusiasm (not orgasm) and allow yourself to be pulled along by sensations, until you feel yourself getting genuinely excited.

4. FANTASISE – KNOW WHAT YOU WANT FROM SEX

Wanting enjoyable sex without knowing exactly what will make it enjoyable places all the responsibility into someone else's hands. Instead of hoping you'll find a lover who'll teach you the tricks of the trade, learn them for yourself. Expand your sexual knowledge by thinking about scenarios that turn you on, and confiding in your friends for tips. Apart from the relief of talking about sex, they'll probably be able to give you some pretty workable tips. Then educate yourself: look through sex books and DVDs, and use the information to boost your sexual knowledge and give you ideas when you next have sex.

5. BE REALISTIC ABOUT SEX

Forget the cinematic climaxes, endless moans and orgasms. It's the quality, not the quantity of sex that you should be concerned with. To sex up your sex life, be realistic about what you expect from sex. If you're with a man who listens to what you're saying about sex, tries to please you in bed and lets you experiment, you're on to a good thing and are pretty guaranteed of upping the sexual ante.

> 'Upping your sexual knowledge really does work when it comes to feeling sexier and more sexually confident. I used to rely on men to tell me what to do to be sexy and it never really worked for me and I didn't really like sex. It wasn't until I read a sex book at the age of 26 (old, I know) that I realised if I wanted to be sexy I had to discover what made me feel sexy and that meant experimenting and speaking up for myself.'
> Zoe, 29

6. FOCUS ON SENSATIONS, NOT A CHECKLIST

When you're having sex, stop thinking. That sounds hard, but you need to switch off the part of your head that worries that you look vile or judges you and makes you think that maybe you're not doing the right thing. To do this start by focusing on your breath, this brings you right back into the present; next, think about what you're experiencing – how does that kiss/touch feel? What's it doing to your body? What's your natural response to this? Keep your eye on the game in hand and you won't have time to worry.

EXERCISE THREE

1. What's your biggest sexual fear?
2. Is this something you've been told or you have assumed about yourself?
3. How can you change the record and work through this?

> **INSTANT NAUGHTY TASK**
> Do something risky for you the next time you're having sex; for example, initiate sex, open the curtains, try a new position, and suggest a new idea!

STEP FOUR

Become a pleasure seeker

Pleasure seekers know that sometimes it doesn't pay to delay gratification and so give in to the pleasures of life's treats whether they are a delicious piece of chocolate, a mouth-watering drink or a pair of exquisite and expensive shoes. If you're adept at savouring those little treats in life, you need to apply the same tactics to your sex life. Sex doesn't have to occur just when the time is right or when someone else initiates it – to get the full pleasure you need to savour it all. The kisses, the flirting, the emails and the physical! Not sure it will work for you? Then experiment and widen your sexual boundaries by:

I. RELAXING ABOUT SEX

To enjoy being sexy, you need to feel that you can deal with whatever happens, embarrassing noises, awkward fumbles, wobbly bits, embarrassed conversations – these are all just part of the rich tapestry of real sex; meaning, don't get caught up in the belief that red-hot sex has to be sensationally smooth and slick. This is not the movies – this is your life and sex doesn't have to be about earth-shattering orgasms, the right words and doing the right thing. It's simply about getting sexy and having fun with someone, getting close to them and getting passionate alongside all the laughs and embarrassing moments.

2. TRYING SOMETHING NEW

This doesn't have to be a new death-defying position or a spot of role play but simply a change of location, a change of day or even a change of lighting. Small changes have a large impact when it comes to sex, and even the smallest tweak can leave you feeling sexier and naughtier than you've done in years. If you're stuck for where to go, ask your partner and see what you can spark in him, as perhaps he's just been waiting for you to ask.

3. BEING PASSIONATE ABOUT EVERYTHING

There's nothing sexier than someone who can light up a room with their personality and zest for life and if that's not you it's easy to make it you by becoming enthusiastic about whatever you choose to do. Yes, do it with gusto whether you're kissing someone goodbye, welcoming someone new, walking across a room, or taking your clothes off. Passion is contagious, as is enthusiasm, so make sure you reek of it.

4. OPENING YOURSELF UP TO FANTASY

You have to think sexy to feel sexy, so if your inner life is bereft of sexual stimulus you need to boost up the internal action. This can be as simple as making yourself think about sex for five minutes a day, talking about sex more often with friends, and opening up your imagination to sexier ideas via books and films. It doesn't have to be pornographic but simply sexy and sensual. It all counts as pleasure and is nothing to feel ashamed about.

5. FORGETTING WHAT EVERYONE ELSE GETS UP TO

Also known as ignore those statistics that talk about how much sex other people are having. Who cares if your neighbours are at it night or day or if your best friend has ten-minute orgasms (unlikely, by the way)? What counts when it comes to sex is what you get up to. If you and your partner feel sexy, satisfied and happy with your sex life then it doesn't matter if you do it once a month or once a day. Likewise, if your idea of naughty sex is sex with the lights on, or sex in the great outdoors, then who cares what others think of that – the aim with sex is always to be true to yourself and there's nothing sexier than that!

INSTANT NAUGHTY TASK
Think of one thing that would give you pleasure right now and do it!

A word about sexiness and coupledom

If you're currently part of a couple and also part of the way through your naughty-but-nice makeover, it pays to be aware of the effect sudden sexiness can have on your relationship. Like finding your confidence, suddenly becoming sexy can throw even the most secure man into a wild-macho-man panic, simply because it can feel threatening and scary to have the woman you love become a sex goddess in the bedroom and a master of flirting at parties. Do it without talking about it first and he may assume you're ripe for an affair, bored with him and simply about to take flight, which is why it pays to be careful about how you flex your new sexiness muscle.

For starters, whereas it's easy to blame your relationship for the death of sexual excitement, the reality is that couples who grow together stay together. So if you're going on a journey of sexual self-discovery, get your partner on board, too. Talk to him about what you're changing and why, and emphasise the benefits this can and will have to your relationship. At the same time talk about your sex life, not only what might need work but also what is working fantastically well, what might work better and what he wants and needs.

Next, experiment together. Discuss what gives you pleasure in and out of bed, and work out how you can generally have more fun together. Think pleasure, think naughtiness and think sexy. Above all, remember there are all kinds of ways to spice up your sex life and banish monotonous sex: new positions and new techniques, but most of all a new attitude. Simply going from someone who sucked in her stomach while having sex and dimmed the lights to someone who races around naked and smiles and laughs throughout is as invigorating and liberating a change as a million new positions.

TEN WAYS TO STAY SEXY TOGETHER

1. Don't stop flirting and trying with each other, no matter how long you've been together.
2. Talk about it when sex goes wrong and when sex goes right.
3. If you don't feel like sex, make it clear you're rejecting sex, not the person.
4. Make an effort to enjoy sex together by putting in some regular effort.
5. Don't dismiss the quickie, especially if you're both time-starved.
6. Do something different sexually at least every third time you have sex.
7. Increase your sexual IQ by staying sexually alert to new information and products.
8. Be a great lover for him, not for your ego, or to keep up with your friends.
9. Stay healthy to keep your sex drive up – exercise, a good diet and less alcohol make for a high sex drive and sexy relationship.
10. Tell each other how attractive and sexy you are, whenever you can and whenever the mood takes you.

Freedom
SEX-BOMB TIPS

When I started writing this chapter I asked a whole load of women for their views on being sexy, and sexiness in general, and got an earful of abuse back from a lot of them. 'What has sex got to do with self-esteem?' said some. 'I thought this was a serious self-esteem book?' said another. 'You're not going to make women feel bad about their sex lives are you?' said someone else. Their antagonism surprised me until I delved further into their questionnaires and read about their war with their body image, and their beliefs about what women can and can't say about their sex lives, desires, wants and needs.

My answer to all of those women is simply that you're fooling yourself if you can't admit that the whole of your life is wrapped up in how you feel about yourself. Which is why learning to be naughty but nice in the sex stakes is simply about discovering how to let go, have more fun and allowing yourself to be the person you know you are inside, whether you're naked in bed with a man, or doing a presentation to 50 people at work.

Sexiness is simply about celebrating your sensual side, the part of you that makes you feel attractive, appealing and gorgeous, so that you can walk into a room and feel like a celebrity, or go out in no make-up and not feel like the whole world is judging you. It's also about having a sexy attitude about yourself so that you don't crumble in the presence of sexier and cooler women or stumble when someone attractive talks to you. Above all it's about embracing sexiness so that you can talk about sex without getting flustered, and have sex without faking it. It's also about not feeling bad that you don't live up to someone else's standards, but feeling sexy so that you can add sex to your list of life's great pleasures – and do it without feeling bad.

1. FEELING SEXY

There are many ways to feel sexy in your daily life, and many of these are to do with the ways you treat yourself. For example, do you have a wardrobe for 'best' and then clothes for the rest of your life? If so, open your closet, pull out those best clothes and start wearing them. Many of us suffer from the clothes-for-best syndrome where we only wear the clothes that make us feel good on special occasions, which, let's face it, are often few and far between. 'Stop waiting, start wearing' should be your new motto, because if you feel sexy, you'll feel confident, good about yourself and happy – so isn't it worth wearing your best as often as possible? Next, think pampering yourself. If your idea of luxury products is a bar of nice-smelling soap, get down to your local chemist and start trying out all the body creams, massages, perfumes and luxury beauty products. You don't always have to go expensive, but using these products will leave you feeling sleek, spoiled and gorgeous. Then be aware of your grooming. You may think you've got no time to look after yourself, but greasy hair, chipped nails, overgrown eyebrows and crumpled clothes all scream 'I don't think much of myself'. Always view yourself as the most valuable product you own, and invest, invest, invest in yourself. How you look in terms of grooming tells the world more than you think about how you feel about yourself and how willing you are to look after yourself (for more on this see the section on Style).

150

2. STAYING SEXY

There are plenty of things in this life that stop us from feeling sexy – tiredness, stress, frustration, illness, general bad health, and even a bad partner. So if you feel that despite your best efforts you still feel as sexy as a brown paper bag you need to do a general overview of your life to determine what it is, or who it is that's squashing your sexiness. Stress is the number-one libido killer, because when you're stressed the body diverts its energy to parts of your body that need refuelling and so your sex drive gets zapped. Likewise tiredness is guaranteed to leave you feeling depressed and down on yourself, and a bad lover who continually sucks away your self-confidence will leave you feeling that you're not good enough. Which is why sexiness has as much to do with how we live our lives as with what we do in our lives. So give yourself a life MOT and work out what needs to change, what needs an overhaul and what needs to be chucked out for good.

If you've done all that and, despite your best efforts, still can't see your sparkle, give yourself a break. We all have what I call bad-hair days (also known as bad-skin days/fat days/blah days and I'm-not-getting-up days) and when this happens, instead of struggling to rise above it, it pays to sink into it and just enjoy it. Let's face it, there's pleasure to be had in donning your most comfortable clothes, lazing about on the sofa, eating ice cream and watching your favourite DVD. Remember: it still counts as pleasure even if you're doing your best impression of a couch potato, plus there will always be other days when you can rev up your sexy engines, vamp up your look and go out and conquer the world!

3. BEING SEXY

The human brain is an amazing tool: it can push you to limitless adventure or help you spiral yourself into the ground. It can also help you to feel you're bland, boring and dull, or sexy, hot and alluring, which is why being sexy is as much about maintaining a positive state of mind as a positive state of well-being. Unsure if you can think yourself sexy? Well, think of the last time someone gave you a compliment out of the blue. How did you suddenly feel about yourself? It's likely you held your head up a bit higher, smiled a little bit more and walked around with a bit more of a spring in your step. That, in a nutshell, is thinking yourself sexy! To do it to yourself all you have to do is look in the mirror and, each time, tell yourself something good before you walk away. Contrary to popular belief this won't make you big-headed or vain (both tend to have more to do with insecurity and low esteem than high esteem) but will reinforce the fact that you are sexy. Do it each time you look in the mirror and it will become second nature, until you start realising that you are the sex bomb you've always dreamed of being.

One-month Sexiness Planner

The aim of this month's planner is to insert major sexiness into your life. This means looking at how you think about sex and your persona and focusing on your thoughts and behaviour.

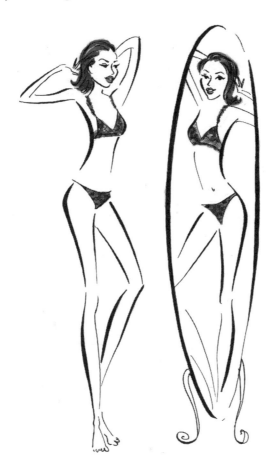

WEEK ONE

Monday   Think about how you perceive yourself on the sexiness scale. Not just in terms of orgasms but verve for life and sensuality. Rate your sensuality and sexuality out of ten.

Tuesday   Think of three things that would make you feel sexier about yourself: (1) something about your physicality; (2) something emotional; and (3) something about your behaviour.

Wednesday   Today put your physical goal into action – either work on getting fit, changing your look or upping your sexual knowledge via books or DVDs.

Thursday   Boost your self-esteem by thinking about your emotional thought patterns. How do you think about yourself in social situations and how do you imagine others see you?

Friday   Make today a pleasure day and choose to find pleasure in every thing you do – from watching TV to going to work. Even if you don't feel it, fake it to make it by acting as if you're filled with pleasure and note how it makes you feel.

Saturday   Consider what makes you feel sexy and what doesn't. Write a list and conjure up a picture of a sexier life for yourself and then work out how you can start living like that.

Sunday   Spend 30 minutes thinking about who you consider to be sexy and why? Go beyond looks and focus on innate sexiness, sexy behaviour and the factors that make people alluring. How can you harness some of this kind of sexiness in your own life?

WEEK TWO

Monday   Think of sex beyond the realms of the physical (i.e. sex) and conjure up what makes you feel sensuous, alluring and attractive. What would you have to do to feel attractive and alluring every day? Put one thought into action.

Tuesday   Ask yourself how could you have a more passionate work life? What would make you feel enthusiastic about your daily life? What could you do to feel more excitement for your work?

Wednesday   Focus on your body language and start working on portraying a sexier vibe via how you talk, move and enter a room. Focus on posture, holding your head high, and not using defensive body language when speaking.

Thursday   How pleasure-starved is your life? Think of four things that make you feel happy and do one every day until the start of next week.

Friday   Consider if you compartmentalise your sexiness into your sex life, your holidays or your weekends. To live a naughtier, sexier life, you need to think and be sexy every day.

Saturday   Rate all your pleasures out of ten and then write off anything that scores six or under and replace it with a new one that revs up your sexiness quota.

Sunday   Have a sexy Sunday and immerse yourself in sexy DVDs, books, food, clothes and people – and see how you feel by the end of the day.

WEEK THREE

Monday   Re-stock your underwear drawer. It sounds ridiculous but treating yourself to naughty but nice undies (remember you define what's sexy so don't just go for the obvious) not only adds a thrill element to your wardrobe but can also make you feel sensual even when you're in the most boring of clothes.

Tuesday   Do something today that rates a ten on your pleasure scale for no other reason than it makes you feel good, and makes you feel naughty but nice!

Wednesday   Be more daring all day. Not just about what you wear but also what you say and how you act. The aim is to get sexy by being naughty, enterprising and audacious.

Thursday   Forget about being perfect. Perfectionism is the kiss of death to a sexy life. Sexy women aren't perfect – they just care less about what others think and focus more on what makes them feel good.

Friday   Take a good look at yourself naked. Stand in front of a mirror and consider all your good points. What makes you feel proud? What are the sexiest parts of your body and what could you do to emphasise these areas?

Saturday   Build a sexy outlook by broadening your sexual horizons. Expand your sexual knowledge, your sexual know-how and your sexual experience by trying three new things this weekend.

Sunday   Go on a charm and flirting offensive. (1) Boost your flirting skills; and (2) put them into action all day. Say 'hello' to strangers, smile at men you fancy and throw out compliments to anyone who passes your way.

WEEK FOUR

Monday Accept every compliment thrown your way this week. Batting them away is a sign of low self-esteem – learn to acknowledge them and file them under 'things to make me feel better'.

Tuesday Remind yourself of all the ways you sparkle in order to zap self-consciousness in social situations. Think about what people like about you the most, what you value in yourself and all the ways you've become a sexier woman.

Wednesday Do you find sex too embarrassing to talk about? If words fail you then get used to talking about sex in general. Discuss it with your girlfriends, discuss it out of bed, and make it a topic that's present in your life so that it becomes part of who you are.

Thursday Be realistic about your sex life. Forget the cinematic climaxes, endless moans and orgasms. To sex up your sex life, focus on what makes you happy in bed, and be realistic about what you expect from sex.

Friday Do something risky for you the next time you're having sex, for example: initiate sex, open the curtains, try a new position or suggest a new idea.

Saturday Sex up your sex life – the reality is, no one is born being good at sex, like any skill it's something we all have to learn, which means wherever you are now on the sexual scale it's more than possible to sex up your life, feel more sexual confidence and exude the allure of a sex goddess.

Sunday Be passionate about everything because there's nothing sexier than someone who can light up a room with their personality and zest for life. So do everything with gusto whether you're kissing someone goodbye, welcoming someone new or walking into a room.

Style

Introduction

If you've ever watched a TV programme or flicked through a magazine and felt green with envy at the seemingly effortless way some women dress and look, you're not alone. Most of us go through life wishing we could walk into a junk shop and come out looking like a million dollars, only to walk into a junk shop and come out looking as if we were a bag lady. Effortless grace, allure, taste, style – when it comes to the final touches to making over your self-esteem this is what you need to live a naughtier life. Why? Well, because what's on the outside affects how you feel on the inside, and vice versa.

The reality is that most of us aren't perfect. We've all got things we don't like about ourselves. Most of us don't look so hot without make-up and brushed hair, and most of us have gripes about our bodies that we've had since we were 13 years old. I would like a longer torso – weird, I know, but in my mind's eye I can see it – non-Martian feet, a nose that doesn't take over in photos. Yet, I can also look in the mirror and see these things in perspective and see that they make up my own unique style, because I've realised that you can't take yourself too seriously when it comes to how you look, and you can't go around like I did for many years believing I'd be happier and wealthier and more fulfilled if only I had smaller breasts, bouncy hair and thinner thighs!

What's more, I realised in the name of living a naughtier and more adventure-filled life that it was more than okay to spend time on your look, and in doing so it didn't detract from your credibility as a person. In fact, as I've said earlier, if you make an effort to look good on the outside it enhances your credibility as a person, because it shows others that you care about yourself. Saying 'I'm beautiful on the inside', doesn't count if what you're actually saying is 'I am not attractive on the outside and that doesn't matter'. Both parts count because both parts influence each other and both parts make up just who you are.

Of course, in a world that does its best to make us obsessed with shopping, owning, needing and wanting, it's easy to get hooked on the idea that to have style you need designer clothes, Botox injections, a size ten body, thin thighs, and expensive shoes. Luckily that's nonsense, because the key to having innate style is to appreciate who you are, make the best of who you are and separate this from what you have, own or need.

> 'What's style – simple: it's about making the most of who you are. Don't blindly follow fashion is my advice. Take a little bit of what you like, a little bit of something fashionable, and adapt it to your body type. The aim is to feel confident and comfortable and happy in how you look.' Julie, 30, Stylist

Quiz

WHAT'S YOUR STYLE?

Are you style-obsessed or style-challenged? Do you feel
fashion rules your life or that being fashionable is beyond
you? If so, don't despair – take this quiz and find out what's
holding you back.

1. **When you look at the contents of your wardrobe,
    what do you see?**
a. Nothing you want to wear. (C)
b. An array of new in-fashion items. (A)
c. A series of T-shirts and pairs of jeans. (D)
d. Old favourites. (B)

2. **If you had to describe your style, it would be:**
a. Up-to-date and in-fashion. (A)
b. Easy and comfortable. (D)
c. Hopeless. (C)
d. Stuck in an era. (B)

3. **What do your friends usually say about your sense of style?**
a. How do you afford all your clothes? (A)
b. Do you wear anything besides jeans? (D)
c. You should wear X and Y. (C)
d. They make fun of it. (B)

4. When you go shopping, you always …

a. Reach for the old familiars. (D)

b. Feel in a panic and buy something you're unlikely to wear. (C)

c. Buy something you've seen a celebrity wearing. (A)

d. You rarely go shopping. (B)

5. What single thing would benefit your look?

a. Someone throwing away all your clothes. (C)

b. Weight loss/weight gain/plastic surgery. (D)

c. More money. (A)

d. Expert advice. (B)

6. What's the one area you often get wrong?

a. You can't work out what suits you and what doesn't. (C)

b. You let fashion dictate your style choices. (A)

c. You don't/won't experiment with clothes. (B)

d. You feel awkward when you have to go smart. (D)

7. If someone compliments you on how you look, you …

a. Feel they are lying and just being nice. (C)

b. Feel surprised. (B)

c. Shrug it off. (D)

d. You think they have taste. (A)

8. What single thing most dictates your sense of style (or lack of it)?

a. Magazines. (A)

b. Your self-esteem. (B)

c. How you used to look. (C)

d. Nothing influences you. (D)

Results

Add up all the answers you gave that were followed by (A) and then those followed by (B), and so on. Then see which score was the highest. If you scored highest on the (A) answers that makes you a Fashion Victim, see below. If you scored highest on the (B) answers that makes you Stuck-in-an-era, and so on.

FASHION VICTIM (mostly As)

Being interested in fashion is one thing, but letting it dominate your style choices is another. Whereas buying the latest thing and wearing the latest style make you fashionable it doesn't make you stylish, because the chances are not everything you buy suits you and not everything you wear fits who you are. What you need to do is delve through your wardrobe – and I am guessing it's a large one – and work out what encapsulates you and who you are. Don't tie yourself to a designer or the look of a celebrity to create a persona; think about what you need to emphasise and cover up, what makes you feel good, sexy and alluring, and what helps you to stand out from the crowd. Style is something unique and personal, so stop thinking about what everyone else is telling you to wear, and consider what it is you want and why.

STUCK-IN-AN-ERA (mostly Bs)

The style experts say many of us are stuck in an era where we were most happy. Ways to know that this is you is if you're still wearing clothes you've had for years and if, when you look at an old photo, you can see yourself in something similar to what you're wearing now. The problem with being stuck in a style era is that it doesn't allow for who you are now and tells people you haven't moved on. Whereas you can take elements from where you used to be and merge them into a new style, it's important to think about what you're trying to say with your look and who it is you want people to see when they look at you. Focus on moving forward with your style by de-cluttering your wardrobe. Remember: you can't be someone new if you're still holding on to who you used to be.

AFRAID OF CLOTHES (mostly Cs)

You'd be surprised at how many people feel completely stumped and stuck when it comes to clothes. So much so that their wardrobes are either stuffed to the brim with purchases they never wear or full of clothes they don't really like but wear anyway. So if shopping fills you with panic, and you're someone who feels they have given up when it comes to fashion, don't despair. Hitting a style rock-bottom means the only way is up, and this section can help you find your confidence to dress better and locate your long-lost style gene without sending you into a hyperventilating panic.

DENIM-GIRL (mostly Ds)

If jeans (or track-pants, or big, loose, baggy jumpers) are your clothing mainstay, it's likely you've just stopped thinking about style, fashion and clothes, whether for peace of mind or pure ease. This isn't a real problem unless you feel thrown and bemused when you're called to dress up and change your look for an event. If so, you need to ask yourself whether you are hiding your light under a bushel or simply opting out of the game because you have no idea where to start. Either way, this section can help you expand your current look and boost your style potential.

Style
FACING THE FACTS

What makes a woman stylish? It's partly something known as allure – a particular pull and magnetism that certain women can pull off by simply walking into a room. These women make you look twice, they make you want to be them and often they make you want to steal all their clothes! Believe it or not, this type of person can be you, because no matter how style-challenged you are right now it's more than possible to find your allure, work out what looks good on you (and what doesn't), and what makes you feel 100 per cent more appealing. And yes, it is important in the naughty-but-nice stakes, because if you work on rebuilding the inside and stoke up your dreams, sexiness and attitude, you need to finish the job by showing you've changed on the outside as well.

Ignore what you look like because you think it's shallow to be concerned with clothes, or you can't be bothered, and it's akin to storing a beautiful diamond in an old newspaper – that is, eventually you're going to start forgetting what's on the inside.

Perfect your style so that you look good, feel good and amaze people when you walk in a room, and it will be a permanent wake-up call to yourself that (1) you've changed; (2) you have confidence; and (3) you are worthy of anything you put your mind to.

So what is style? Style, in a nutshell, is what makes you stand out from the crowd and boosts your own confidence tenfold. It's about more than clothes and grooming, although what you wear and how you look after yourself is vital here – it's basically an expression; meaning, it's how you choose to show yourself to the world, to your loved ones, and even to yourself. It doesn't (or rather it shouldn't) come from fashion pages, shop windows or shopping sprees but from knowing who you are and how to make the best of yourself and your body shape. So, worry not if you currently have the style and panache of a bag lady and have been dressing to disappear for years, this section can help you find your captivating spirit.

STEP ONE

WARNING – style-free zone ahead!

Clothes are not just there to cover you up and make you look anonymous. If anything, what you wear, how you look and the way you look after yourself should lift your spirits and inspire you in everyday life. It sounds a weird concept if you've never put that much effort or thought into your clothes and grooming, but the fact remains that whatever you're wearing is part of who you are and should help to make you feel brave, sexy, confident and definitely naughty but nice. If your clothes don't make you feel like that then it's likely you're either wearing the wrong clothes for your shape or simply not making enough effort with your personal style.

Being a latecomer to the world of style, it would be true to say that for years I was the perpetual woman in black. Back when I had 18kg (40lb/2 stone 12lb) to lose, I wore black for its slimming effect, but then post-weight loss I wore it for the anonymity it gave me and the sense of classic chic I felt it instilled in my look. The problem was it didn't make me look cool and classic but did make me look anonymous. So, naturally, as my confidence grew there did come a time when I was eager to branch out and change my style. Unfortunately, by the time that happened I just didn't feel I could do it because I had no idea what suited me and why.

And that's the problem with style. If you spend years covered up and hiding away, when you do decide to get stylish and get a new look it's like walking into a foreign country. I would go into shops, stare blankly at clothes and styles that other women seemed to buy and put together with relative ease, and simply leave with yet another black T-shirt. When I did experiment I'd inevitably get it wrong and walk around feeling awkward and alien instead of transformed and glamorous.

Then I bumped into a friend who seemed to have transformed herself overnight into an amazingly stylish woman, and, when I asked her how, it turns out she had 'had her colours done'. Which basically meant that she went to see a professional stylist who specialised in colour and found out what shades and clothes suited her. Being the eternal cynic, I made lots of fun of her, and then shamefacedly asked for the expert's number. Not quite believing that anyone specialising in colour or clothes could have an effect on how I looked, I then sat with the stylist for two hours and literally saw the impact that getting style right could have, not just on my look but in how I felt about myself.

I also discovered, much to my joy and bank account, that black was actually one of my colours and that in amongst the wrong clothes, weird fabrics and odd styles I was wearing, there were a few things I was getting right. On the whole, though, I needed to be bolder, more courageous and basically get out there and try on a lot of things in shop changing rooms. Now I'm a different person when it comes to working out what to wear and buy. I'll pile into a dressing room loaded with clothes of varying sorts, even things I am 100 per cent sure will look terrible. I ask shop assistants for advice, and when I look at my reflection, instead of immediately thinking about what others will think, I consider what I think and how the clothes make me feel.

Opting for something as simple as a change of colour did, literally, change my look overnight, and once I'd got over the initial idea that 'everyone was looking at me' (which of course they weren't) and the barrage of compliments about my new look, I actually realised my new look was boosting my confidence and allowing the real me to show her true colours (excuse the pun). So now I have trousers that make me feel smart and sophisticated, jeans that make me feel sexy, tops that inspire me to flirt and jackets that make me feel confident – and shoes galore that do the whole of the above and more (for more on finding your colour see Step Two, Try on New Hats in the Style Rehab section).

So, my point is, as depressing as your own style might feel now, don't despair and assume that you can't do it, because when it comes to style everyone's got it, and sometimes all you have to do is dig deep and let it fight its way out.

Naughty-but-nice living is as much about style as it is about attitude, because if you can let go and dress for yourself and not hide your fears and anxieties, and stop worrying about what others think, you'll feel free to express who you are, no matter what others say. So step one towards better style is to simply stop shopping. A weird thing to say, I know, when later I am actually going to encourage you to shop selectively, but right now by 'stop shopping' I mean take the focus off consumerism, wanting and needing, as this prevents you from thinking about what it is you really want to achieve with your style. Next, head to your wardrobe and get ready to throw things away. Feng shui theories aside, it's hard to come up with new ideas about style when your head and room are still cluttered with reminders of what you're trying to get away from. So take a long, hard look at what you own:

EXERCISE ONE

1. Are you holding on to clothes that say more about who you used to be than who you want to be, and who you are now? If so, chuck them out.
2. Are you holding on to items that you feel one day you'll either feel like wearing again or will fit into again? Again, throw them away.
3. Are you holding on to items that you don't wear just because they're in fashion or someone bought them for you or they were expensive? If so eBay them so that you can actually make some money to buy new clothes from the proceeds.

As hard as it is, try not to be sentimental about your clothes. If in doubt ask yourself why you're keeping them, and if you haven't got two good reasons, throw them out. The reality is that most of us have way too many clothes – the result of fickle buys, overspending and generally not de-junking as we go along. So if you can't de-clutter, enlist the help of a good friend, preferably one that's been on at you for years to change your style (this makes her more ruthless in the face of your reluctance). Once you've cleaned up, give yourself a deadline for those recycling bags, otherwise you'll be rifling through them in no time. The best bet is to give yourself 24 hours, and, after that, anything that you feel 100 per cent tied to pull out of the bag, and send the rest to a charity shop.

> **INSTANT NAUGHTY TASK**
> **Unsure of whether to throw something out – remember if you're even considering it, it should go.**

STEP TWO

Look at your body

Yes, we're back to body image, because, let's face it, how you feel about your body directly corresponds to how you look after yourself and what you choose to wear. So, hands up if you're guilty of compartmentalising your body and not seeing yourself as a whole? Take Gina, 28, who, when asked what she sees when she looks in the mirror said, 'Great eye-lashes'. True, she has amazing long and lush lashes but she also has a great face, long legs and a winning smile. However, in Gina's book her face is 'spoilt' by her 'lopsided mouth'. Her legs are wrong because 'they are out of proportion to my body' and, she adds, 'my teeth ruin my smile'. As a result, Gina wears baggy jeans to disguise her legs, rarely smiles without covering her mouth and can't see what she looks like as a complete package. Her warped perspective occurred at 16 years old when she went along to audition for a model agency and was given the above verdict on

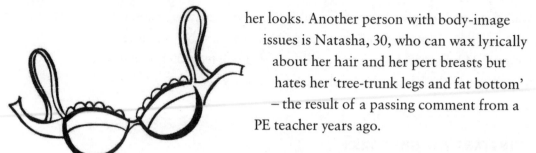

her looks. Another person with body-image issues is Natasha, 30, who can wax lyrically about her hair and her pert breasts but hates her 'tree-trunk legs and fat bottom' – the result of a passing comment from a PE teacher years ago.

My point here is that if you have a love–hate relationship with your body, it's likely you (1) rarely look at yourself as a whole in the mirror; and (2) only see yourself in terms of what you like and what you loathe, which is why the first step in finding your style is to take a long, hard look at who you really are.

EXERCISE TWO

What negative comments are you holding on to from people such as your parents, ex-partners, and so on, that you have allowed to define you?

1. Are the above beliefs you've been telling yourself real or have you just been mindlessly repeating them?

2. What benefits have you got from telling yourself your beliefs are true? Has it allowed you to opt out of trying or given you a reason to cover up?

3. Stand in front of a mirror in your underwear and take a long, hard look at your body, and see yourself as a whole. Note what's good, what's not so bad and what new positive beliefs you can start building about your body.

It's vital to appraise your shape in a positive way, because until you see your body as a shape with potential it's hard to think about dressing yourself well and making the most of your personal style. Clothes need to accentuate what you have, as well as disguise, flatter and show off your pros, so you need to be able to evaluate your body realistically so that you can dress in the best way possible. Of course, interpreting your shape in a positive way isn't easy if, in your mind, you want to look like a 1.8m (5ft 10in) gazelle and in reality you're 1.6m (5ft 2in) with lots of round edges. So, when you look at your true shape try to leave your preconceptions on the floor with your clothes and ask yourself:

- Are you pear-shaped, as in heavy around the bottom and hips and small around the breast and arm area?
- Are you apple-shaped – heavy round the middle with no waist?
- Are you top-heavy?
- Are you flat-chested?
- Are you straight up and down?
- What are your ankles and calves like?
- Are your upper arms chunkier than your wrists?

All these factors can help you determine your body's pros and cons, because for every con there is a corresponding pro that you can balance out your body with.

For example:

- If you're flat-chested, the chances are you have a lean upper body and nice arms, and you can wear sexy tops and show off your arms.
- If you're top-heavy, it's likely that whereas you have wobbly batwing arms, a noticeable tummy and breasts, you also have long legs

(proportionately, to your body), slim hips and a small bottom that can be dressed up to make you look longer and leaner.

- If you have chunky ankles, go for long boots to sex up your leg.

Once you have your body in check you can start looking at your current wardrobe to see if your clothes accentuate your good bits or your bad bits. Again, throw out anything that seems to make your bad bits worse (a good friend can be an excellent aid here). And remember the basic rules:

1. Clothes that are too baggy and unfitted make you look bigger.
2. Clothes that are too tight make you look uncomfortable.
3. Trousers that are slightly loose (as opposed to hanging off your bottom) make you look leaner.
4. A good bra is the key to a good look.
5. Tight support knickers should fit well, not create an extra spare tyre at your stomach.
6. Too much colour in one go isn't a good thing.
7. If in doubt ask a shop assistant for advice and help.

INSTANT NAUGHTY TASK
Go into a shop and try on two things you like but you'd never usually wear. Note how they make you feel and in what ways they make you feel good/sexy/different about yourself.

STEP THREE

Silence the critic within

Of course, the true key to style is not to follow fashion blindly but to start appreciating what you have to offer and taking some risks and chances. Sounds fantastic, doesn't it? But you're probably asking how the heck do you do that. Well, firstly, you have to work on diminishing your self-loathing and judgments; that is, silence the critic within. This is the voice that constantly tells you you're not good enough, you don't deserve things and that you can't be happy/stylish/adventurous until you're perfect.

Most of us have these voices, but some are definitely louder than others, and if that sounds familiar, it's likely that your style is definitely being hindered by the voice that won't let you try. Take Anna, 28. She is amazing to look at, she has dark hair, an enviable hourglass figure and could pass for a 1940s pin-up, yet, most of the time she can be found in very un-sexy jeans and plain T-shirts that are baggier than a circus tent.

'There are days when I look in the mirror and can see what everyone else is talking about when they say I look good, but mostly I feel embarrassed about my body. I grew up in a very strict religious household and from the moment I hit puberty my mum would make me cover up and talk to me about how men would take advantage. She was only doing what she thought was right, but I think my shame about how I look stems from then. On top of that I hit my twenties just as the skinny, wispy look came in, and for years just felt unstylish and wrong. It's only now I am battling that voice in my head and seeing my plus points. It's a hard daily struggle,

EXERCISE THREE

1. What things do you tell yourself you can't have, do or wear?
2. What do you think has or hasn't happened in your life because of your appearance?
3. What would it take for you to feel good about yourself now?

but I actually bought a fitted top the other day. It's such a small move for most women but a massive one for me.'

If you have a loud and vitriolic critic in your head that tells you things about your look and your body, bear in mind that it's created from all your experiences and can be the voice of your parents, friends, past lovers and even things you read in the media. To silence it and balance it out you need to argue back. Don't be someone who negates compliments and stores up the abuse or who chooses to believe something bad someone says because they are being 'honest', and ignore something good because that person's just being 'nice'.

It takes true style and a naughtier attitude to be able to disregard people's criticisms and your own, and feel good about who you are. This can be done on a day-by-day basis, by simply making yourself argue with your internal voice. Help yourself by:

- Questioning every negative thought that comes into your head when you look at yourself in the mirror. Is the thought true or based on someone else's opinion? Why are you being so brutal with yourself and what are you getting from holding yourself back?
- Coming up with a positive for every negative. Your critic says you look silly trying so hard; your voice says you look fantastic making an effort. Your critic says you should stick to what you know; your voice says I'm bored with what I know.
- Overriding your critic. The more times you ignore it and forge ahead, trusting your gut over your worries and anxieties about changing, the quieter and quieter the voice will become, until it disappears.

INSTANT NAUGHTY TASK
The next time your critic butts in – ignore it and do the very opposite of what it's suggesting.

STEP FOUR

Being authentic – living by your own rules

Another major component of style is authenticity. This is the ability to display to the world who you are inside. Of course, it's hard to be authentic and genuine, especially in a world that's eager for everyone to look the same. Being authentic is even more complicated when you don't know who you are, and just don't feel comfortable with change. This is why, as important as your style is, it's also important to stay light-hearted over style issues. Fretting for hours about your look in front of a mirror, and fighting back the tears in shop changing rooms, is not the way to find your style. Having fun with clothes, hair, make-up and accessories, and experimenting with different looks is closer to the answer.

Likewise, style is supposed to be something that you find enjoyable and life inspiring, so don't become someone who feels she has to be seen in the right clothes in case others deem you uncool, or someone who has to have the latest designer bag/shoes/dress so that you feel stylish and in fashion. Similarly, try not to follow fashion blindly or take the advice of friends who seem to know what they're doing and then try to turn you into a mini version of them. True style is authentic; meaning, it should reflect who you are, your personality and the things you love and like in life. To find what's real and genuine for you, ask yourself the questions in the following exercise.

EXERCISE FOUR

1. What do you want people to think when they look at you?
2. What part of your personality, creativity and life could you bring out in your clothes?
3. What image do you see for yourself?

For example, here are the answers for Anna, 28:

What do you want people to think when they look at you?

'Here's a woman who looks like she knows who she is in life and is confident enough to wear something even if it's not in fashion.'

What part of your personality, creativity and life could you bring out in your clothes?

'I would like people to see that I'm interesting. I work a lot with colour (I'm a web designer) and so would like to get away from black and wear brighter, more eye-catching shades.'

What image do you see for yourself?

'Something casual, because I like jeans, but also classic so I don't look studenty and frumpy, but sexy.'

Once you have your answers, the next step is to go shopping and have a look at what's out there. Think of what shops work for you and which ones don't. What styles feel right to you (whether you'd wear them or not)? Above all, educate yourself about clothing terms; that is, know your boot-cut from your hipster, and your empire line from your bias-cut dress, so you can determine what suits your shape and what doesn't. If you're stuck, ask assistants, read up on things, and inform yourself the way you would if you were about to buy a new car.

Once you're loaded up with information, if you still feel you can't move forward, work out what's holding you back. In most cases it's simply a fear of change. We all have clothes that we throw on that make us feel comfortable, that hide our lumps and bumps and allow us to feel safe, and suddenly wearing something new changes that and makes us feel vulnerable and exposed, and open to criticism in an arena that we have previously opted out of. This is hard stuff and can feel strange and diffi-cult at first. Personally, I remember the first time I stopped wearing black and went to a party in a red top – the comments I received were all posi-tive but it was excruciating to be in the limelight, and I spent the whole night wanting to wrap the curtain around myself. If this is your fear, take it slowly. You don't have to transform yourself all at once. Take baby steps, go slowly and take your time to work out who the new stylish you is going to be.

INSTANT NAUGHTY TASK
Throw away one item from your comfy collection. It's a tough one but instantly liberating!

I used to have a T-shirt that I loved, and even when it ripped under the arms I sewed it up and wore it and wore it. I liked to think it was shabby-chic but really I looked like an ageing student in it. One day on the spur of the moment I decided that enough was enough, and I ripped it apart and threw it away. After my initial 'OH MY GOD WHAT WILL I WEAR

NOW!' I opened my wardrobe and made myself find something new and improved to wear. There's nothing like no choice to make you change your ways!

Style Rehab
MAKEOVER TIME!

If you love and adore all those TV programmes where experts take a poor downtrodden and weather-beaten woman and, in the space of 60 minutes, turn her life around, and boost her self-esteem with a spectacular makeover, you're not alone. These programmes are amazingly successful and popular because they home into the simple idea that inside us all lies someone sexier, more beautiful and simply more stylish than the current person trolling about the house in track-pants and a baggy jumper. The message from these shows is simply it could be you! And this is what this section is all about, because I'm about to show you how it could be you with less effort and money than you think!

STEP ONE

Purge the old you

I have a friend who rails hard against any style change, claiming she's happy the way she is, she has her own distinct style and really everyone should leave her alone. We would, except the reality is she is constantly down on herself, criticises her lack of adventure on the clothing front and is essentially stuck in a 1980s time warp. Currently she's experiencing a bit of a comeback but the fact remains she dresses as if she were still 14 and she's now in her thirties. Cute, you may be thinking, but you wouldn't say that if you saw her big teased hair, large earrings and short ra-ra-style skirts. She's the essence of what a stylist friend of mine calls a woman 'stuck in an era'.

The idea here is when it comes to style there's a theory that we all stick to a point in time when we were most happy with our body and look – and for my friend that's definitely 14 years old. Sadly, whereas it is possible to bring elements of the old into the new, you do also have to let go of who you used to be, in order to become who you want to be.

> **'Oh my god, I was really living in an era – the early 1990s – I look at pictures from a few years ago and I see big hair, ugly jewellery and even shoulder pads. Change has been good for me because it's allowed me to let go of the past and be who I am now'. Judy, 28**

So, having chucked away the old you from your wardrobe (and if you haven't, go back to Style, Facing the Facts) now's the time to purge the old you once and for all and think about your body, your look and your life, and to consider what you hope to get from changing your style. Hopefully, your answer appears somewhere in the range of choices that cover more self-esteem, more confidence, more compliments and more satisfaction. So use the following rules to find the new and improved stylish you.

EXERCISE ONE

1. **Rule one** Do it now – as in don't put off changing your style until you're thinner, richer or have had plastic surgery. You can change your look right now, this instant, by simply making a decision to do something you've been considering for ages. Maybe this is a haircut, a change in make-up, a new colour, and/or a new combination of clothes. Perhaps some retail therapy is on the cards or it's time to raid your best friend's wardrobe for the night.

2. **Rule two** Get creative, as in think outside of the box. It's no good throwing your wardrobe contents out, as one friend recently did, and going out there and replacing everything with identical items. If you're scared that you'll comfort-buy and find yourself gravitating towards the tried and tested all the time, take your most brutal friend with you, and ensure she holds on to your purse while you shop. Your aim with finding some naughty style is to be creative and develop your own ideas about style. Don't just read fashion magazines and shop; take a long, hard look at people in your life. Who's style do you most admire and why? Which famous people do you find yourself searching for in magazines, and what is it about their look that you like and admire? Could you steal some of their style tricks, and make them your own,

or adapt a friend's look and make it work on you? You won't know if you don't try.

3. **Rule three** Ask for advice. This is the very thing that most people in a style crisis don't do. Believe it or not, sometimes your mother does know best and your best friend can tell what suits you, and your partner can work out what your best feature is. Allow others some input (although obviously don't let them dictate your look). One fun thing to do is to pick three people and go shopping with them all (or stand in front of your wardrobe with them) and allow them to choose a look for you. The aim here is to see how others view you and how a different input can influence your style. Once they've styled you, ask them why they've put you in certain things and then work out if it's something you think works and something you can adapt into your new look.

4. **Rule four** Don't try to live with a foot in both worlds. Whereas it's tempting and sensible to bring something from the old you into the new, naughtier you, don't try to straddle both worlds; meaning, you won't be able to find your new style if you run back to the comfort of your old style every time it feels difficult or too hard. Not only is it confusing to the mind, but it will also lead you to getting confused about what you're doing and why. Persevere for at least a month and stay away from the old you until then, as it takes four weeks for new patterns to cement.

Before you go in search of your new styles, erase comments such as: 'I'm too old/too fat/too thin/too shy to wear that!' This is a variation on the theme of the critic within, and is also the result of messages from our pasts. Whereas it's true to say that certain styles look better on some people than others, on the whole nothing should be out of bounds to you until you try it.

STEP TWO

Try on new hats

Remember the time when dressing up was fun? Okay so you were seven years old at the time and didn't care what you looked like, because you were in for the sheer enjoyment of it all, but that's how you should feel about clothes now. Trying things on shouldn't be something you do through gritted teeth but something that's pleasurable and gratifying. If it isn't, you're never going to relax enough to find a look you love.

'I look back at pictures of myself as a teenager and I think, where did I get the guts to wear that? Back then I had nasty pink glasses, and would happily wear high heels and short socks or tight tops and really baggy jeans. I looked terrible, but then I look at my face and I always looked happier than I do now. These days I worry all the time about how I look and try really hard and never get close to looking as confident as I did back then.' Jenni, 26

One way to combat this is to get out there and try on lots of hats (well, not literally hats, but you get my drift). When finding a new style your aim should be to keep it simple and then pay special attention to the details; for example, colour, accessories, and, more importantly, what the clothes are saying about you. Remember, less is more, and ban anything you feel in your gut just doesn't suit you.

Firstly, think about colour, because it's key to finding your style. You need to understand what colours suit you and what don't, because often it's the shade of what you wear that makes you appear confident and attractive rather than the garment itself. Colour has power, and if you don't believe me think about how you respond to colour in everyday life. Would you buy soap powder that was bright orange, or the iPod if it just came in beige?

Colour can lift your mood, change how others respond to you and make you feel confident when you're nervous inside, as well as sexy when you feel a bit dull about yourself. To find your best shades, the aim is to find a colour that complements your hair, skin tone and eyes.

Secondly, think about shapes. Having determined what body shape you have in Style, Facing the Facts, Step Two, Look at Your Body, work out areas of your body that you need to emphasise and the areas you need to minimise with your clothes, focusing on balance over everything.

For example:

- Legs: if you have thick calves don't wear skinny heels because they only emphasise the width of your calves; go for a chunkier heel.

EXERCISE TWO

The best way to find which colours best suit you is to stand in front of a mirror in good light and place different items of clothing with different colours around your neckline. Make sure you do one colour at a time, and watch for subtle changes in your skin tone and look.

- Which colours lift your face and which don't?
- Which ones automatically make you feel brighter?
- Which shades bring out the colour of your eyes?

Use a wide selection of colours, from bright and cool shades to warm tones, yellows, reds, and black and white.

If you have slim ankles try a shoe with an ankle strap to accentuate the leanness of your ankle, but if you have thick ankles opt for boots.

- Bust: if you have a large bust, avoid anything that skims over the breasts making a tentlike billowing effect below. Go fitted and structured and opt for V-necks over high necks and round necks.
- Wobbling tummies: choose fabrics and tops that gather in folds around your tummy rather than those that cling.
- Batwing arms: avoid sleeveless tops, especially if your arms end in delicate wrists, as your arms will look out of balance.
- Top-heavy: elongate your legs and make sure your jackets stop at your hips, not your waist or over your bottom.
- Bottom-heavy: choose trousers that skim your bottom and legs, and don't cling or hang too loosely.

Thirdly, accessorise wisely. This is an area many people go OTT in, and whereas you can display your more creative style tendencies with shoes, bags and jewellery, the rules of balance, colour and style apply here as before. If you're large on top, delicate finery just disappears, if you're small on top, large necklaces swamp you. The same goes for bags and scarves.

INSTANT NAUGHTY TASK
Go into a shop and get a shop assistant to help style you for an event.

STEP THREE

Grooming

Beauty is in the eye of the beholder, but if you look in the mirror and are repulsed by what you see then it's likely you are lacking on the beauty style front. The good news is that you don't have to become a beauty bore to have some beauty style, but if your self-esteem has been in the dumper of late, it's likely your beauty/grooming routine has been literally more naughty than nice! This is something that's more common than you think because when you're down on yourself most women take one of two approaches to beauty:

- Approach one: the I-don't-care-approach! Are you someone who can't stand to shave her legs, take off her make-up or have her hair cut? Is soap and water your best beauty tool? If that sounds familiar it's also likely you don't like pampering your body or even having someone else touch it.
- Approach two: the I-spend-a-fortune-on-my appearance-approach! How much time and money do you spend each week on your appearance? It's likely it's quite a lot because you're the queen of facials, expensive creams and luxury spa treatments.

Both approaches are different sides of the same coin, because beauty, although being something you can enjoy, shouldn't take over your whole life (and your bank account), neither should it be so far down your list of priorities that you don't even consider it when you wake up in the morning. A certain amount of grooming is essential when it comes to style, because how you appear to the world indicates how much you value yourself. If you don't believe me, consider how you would feel if you were faced with a woman with dirty teeth, lank hair and a grubby face – an exaggerated example (I hope), but you get my drift. Likewise, how would you feel if you met a woman layered in make-up? Probably equally horrified. Do too much and it smacks of trying to cover up to the world; do too little and you're telling people you don't care about yourself.

To improve your beauty style you simply need to get used to living in your skin, and one way to do this is to focus on a healthy look and a healthier attitude to your beauty routine.

EXERCISE THREE

1. Is your diet and exercise routine up to scratch? What could you do to improve it?
2. In what ways could you pump up your beauty routine so that you felt good when you looked at your reflection, or in which ways could you tone it down so that you worried less about how you looked all the time?
3. Consider three changes to your beauty style and implement them for a week. Note the changes in your look and your feelings about yourself.

If you're a beauty non-doer, possible changes could include:

- Giving up smoking and cutting back on drinking.
- Wearing sunscreen.
- Cleansing and moisturising once a day.
- Exercising three times a week for 60 minutes.
- Drinking eight glasses of water every day.
- Cutting back on coffee.
- Sleeping eight hours a night.

If you're a beauty over-doer, possible changes could include:

- Cutting back by half on the time you spend on beauty products each week.
- Having a bathroom cabinet clear out.
- Spending no more than an hour a day on your beauty routine (including a bath).
- Implementing a healthier lifestyle over a beauty-product lifestyle.
- Allotting the time and resources that you used to spend on grooming to a different area of your life.

STEP FOUR

Hair – make it the crowning glory of your new style

Take a long, hard look at your hairstyle. Are you donning a hairstyle that you haven't changed since you were a teenager? If so, you're not alone, while we all quite happily change everything else in our lives as time goes by, most of us stick to tried-and-tested hairstyles because (1) we can't be bothered to change; and (2) we're not sure how to change. Yet, when it comes to style nothing will radically change your look as much as a decent haircut. Take a look at all those makeover shows; yes they may have had plastic surgery or be wearing clothes that are worth thousands, but the factor that most affects how they look and how stylish they appear is their hair. One decent haircut and you can make up for a lifetime of styling sins.

To get the real thrill of a decent haircut that makes you feel sexy and alluring, you first need to find a hairdresser you gel with. In my time I've had hairdressers I couldn't understand, hairdressers who listened and then ignored what I said and hairdressers that simply couldn't cut hair. As a result I have had some truly awful haircuts, such as a crew cut with shaved patches on the side, a candyfloss-styled curly job and strange red highlights that criss-crossed my head like disco strobe lights. Thankfully, these days I have the most wonderful hairdresser, who not only cuts my hair fantastically well but also is someone I like and trust, and who understands who I am, that's the key to finding your perfect haircut.

Make sure your hairdresser is someone who understands you and likes you, and you're guaranteed to end up with the perfect style because he/she will do their best to create a look that not only suits your face but your lifestyle and your general style. At the same time spend as much time looking after your hair as you do styling it and you'll have healthy, glossy hair that bounces like the TV adverts. Back in the days when my hair was literally falling apart I would spend heaps of money on shampoo and conditioning products and then go out all night, cheat myself out of sleep and eat junk food and wonder why the products didn't work.

Finally, be aware that for a style that counts it doesn't have to be dramatic, as sometimes a small adjustment to the texture (I went from curly to straight) or with the colour can be amazing and life changing. I know women who have gone from long to short who look like they are ten years younger, and others who have gone from ponytails to styled hair and now look like movie stars. Believe me, let your hair be your crowning glory and you'll ooze buckets of naughty style. Here's how:

I. SEE A PROFESSIONAL HAIRDRESSER

We've all had a dodgy haircut where a hairdresser doesn't listen to what we're saying and literally chops off too much or gives us a hairstyle we could never replicate at home, or a colour job that wears us, which is why most people are so distrustful of letting anyone else choose their hairstyle. Thankfully, there is a multitude of ways to find a style that suits you without letting anyone get too scissor-happy with you.

2. WORK OUT YOUR FACE SHAPE

Pull your hair off your face and look in the mirror and trace the shape of your reflection with a lipstick (better still get a friend to do it). This will give you an Oval, Round, Square, Diamond, or Heart shape and that's your face shape. Above all remember, if you're looking to disguise your face shape you can't change it unless you take your hair length above the jaw line.

3. EXPERIMENT

This is easier than you think. If you have curly, hair opt for a straight blow-dry to see what you would look like. If you have straight hair, get your hair curled with tongs or set wavy. Scared of colour? Use a wash-in and wash-out shade to determine what you would like.

4. THINK ABOUT WHAT YOU WANT YOUR HAIRSTYLE TO SAY

Do you want something easy and simple to do or something that screams glamour? This is where a good hairdresser can help you. Talk about what you want and, more importantly, what you don't want, and don't let yourself be bullied into something. In the same way that you wouldn't let someone pick your clothes style, don't let someone pick your hairstyle. Information is power here, so make sure your hairdresser is clear about what you're looking for and you're clear about what he or she's doing.

5. THINK ABOUT YOUR INVESTMENT TIME

Always aim for a style that uses one product and one styling aid, so that your hair looks as if you haven't used anything on it and a colour that doesn't wear you. On top of that the experts say that if your hair takes more than 15 minutes to do, you're overstyling. What's more, if you can't get the look you had in the salon, your style is too high-maintenance so go back and get a cut that suits you. Hair should be enjoyable not sufferable!

6. LOOK AFTER YOUR HAIR HEALTH

Like your skin and your internal health, the state of your hair is not just affected by how many trips you take to the hairdressers but what you put into your body and how you protect it in the sun. To make it the

EXERCISE FOUR

Look at your hair in natural sunlight:

1. **How does it appear to you?** Is it glossy, shiny or dry and brittle? Does the colour do your face justice or is it at odds with everything else about you?

2. **Feel your hair** Is it sticky and loaded with products or left to its own devices? Now take a strand and stretch it. Healthy hair should stretch about a third of its length before it breaks. If it snaps instantly – your hair is damaged or you're lacking in nutrients.

3. **Check the condition** Limp, greasy or lank hair that needs product and hairspray to make it look bouncy is not healthy hair. Whatever your hair type, hair should always be healthy looking and able to hold a style for longer than an hour. If not, you've either got product overload – that is, you're not rinsing your hair out properly after washing – or your scalp is too greasy or too dry. If you have split ends, this is also a sign that the hair is dehydrated and has lost moisture and protein.

crowning glory of your new style you need to treat it with care. Here's how:

To help your hair look and feel healthy, eat hair-friendly produce, such as foods that are rich in omega-3 and 6 essential fatty acids (EFAs). These are fantastic for your hair, as a deficiency in essential oils appears as hair loss, lifeless hair, dandruff and brittle hair. Omega-3 is found in oily fish – tuna, mackerel, salmon – and in walnuts, and dark-green leafy vegetables; omega-6 is found in nuts and seeds, especially linseed, pumpkin and sesame seed oils and also in evening primrose oil. Also eat vitamin B-based foods – these are not only needed to convert the omega oils in the body but also support protein in the hair. Vitamin B can be found in brown bread, brown rice, oats and eggs. Finally, opt for antioxidants – vitamins A, C and E. These help protect the hair from free radicals, such as daily pollutants, and improve hair growth and condition. Eat dark-green veggies, citrus fruits and avocados.

INSTANT NAUGHTY TASK
If you want to grow your hair, first try on some wigs in a department store to see if long hair would suit you. Try on a short wig if you fancy changing from long to short hair.

STEP FIVE

Make-up

Is your make-up bag a pick-and-mix delight of beauty-counter free gifts, and shades and brands you've been wearing since you were a teenager? If it is, you're not alone. When it comes to make-up most women tend to stick to what they know even if what they know was garnered back when they were 14 years old. Like hairstyles, your make-up style can make or break your look, and it will tell someone a lot about the kind of person you are.

Think of it this way: if you came across a woman who is plastered with make-up what would you think of her? Would her look shout confidence

---

EXERCISE FIVE

1. Open up your make-up bag and lay out all the products you have on the table, dividing them into make-up you use and make-up you don't. Throw out anything older than two years old, as it will either have gone off or no longer suit you.
2. Consider what your make-up says about you. Do people notice you more or less when you wear make-up? Have people commented on the amount of make-up you wear? Could you go out bare faced and be happy about it?
3. What changes could you make to improve your make-up style?

and heaps of self-worth to you or would you assume she was maybe a little insecure and hiding something? What if someone was wearing zero make-up? Would you assume they were happy in their skin or too lost to do anything about themselves?

Make-up, if you choose to wear it, can help boost your confidence, change your look and improve your feelings about yourself, simply because, like clothes, it can maximise your pluses and minimise your weaker points. However, like a good hairstyle, make-up is a surface mender; meaning, to look and feel truly fabulous you need to look after your insides just as much as your outside and drink plenty of water (at least eight glasses a day), wear sunscreen (nothing less than factor 15) and eat nutritious food that's rammed with vitamins. Get that right and you're creating a perfect palette on which to create any look you want, plus avoiding having to use make-up as a cover-up for flaws such as wrinkles and spot trouble that make you feel insecure about yourself.

To help yourself get your make-up right:

- **Always consider your age and skin type when opting for in-season colours and new products. One type doesn't suit all, and, as with clothes, you need to follow your own path to find a make-up brand and colour that suits you and your skin tone and your lifestyle.**
- **Don't stick to one brand. In the same way that you wouldn't just buy clothes in one shop, you shouldn't just buy make-up from one brand, despite what the sales-counter girls tell you. Mix and match, and bear in mind that expensive brands aren't always better than cheaper ones.**

- Ask an expert to give you a makeover but hold on to your purse. The aim here is to give you an idea, so don't feel coerced into buying; instead, say you need to see what it looks like in the light and give yourself an hour with it on. If you like the look after that, go back and purchase what you fancy.
- Blend and balance. As with your clothes, make-up needs to balance with what you're wearing; that is, don't go bright if you're wanting a casual look and don't go minimal if you're dressing up. More importantly, good make-up should blend with your skin tone (don't let it sit on your jaw line), and when you look in the mirror it should appear natural.

INSTANT NAUGHTY TASK
Go up to your favourite beauty counter and ask if they have any samples you can try at home to see if they suit you. In 99 per cent of cases you'll have a good sample to create a new look from without paying through the nose.

Freedom
BE WHO YOU WANT TO BE

When I think of the stylish women I admire the most, I think of women who are fun. I also think of women who are likeable, easy-going, happy to be who they are and even happier to display that fact to the world. I think of my friends, some of whom wouldn't be seen dead without their lipstick just because having plump lips makes them feel good, and others who happily face the world make-up free because they can't be bothered to wear anything more than sunscreen. I also think of the women I know who are exquisitely dressed and spend lots of time and energy thinking about what to wear because they view it as an extension of themselves, and others who do the opposite but look just as amazing. The unifying factor for all these women is that they have style and a sense of naughtiness because they believe in themselves.

To be honest, most of it didn't come easy to them and, just like most of us struggling to reach our goals and feel better about ourselves, they've undergone a self-esteem makeover of the naughty-but-nice kind. And in the end they have style, not because they're the best dressed or the sexiest or the thinnest, but because they have learned how to be comfortable in their own skins. They make fashion mistakes (who doesn't?), some aren't even in fashion, and whereas others are the epitome of taste, when you meet them you can't deny they all have that enviable ability to hold their heads up and say 'This is who I am!'

What has this got to do with living a naughtier life? Well, the fact is that if you can't let rip and let go with something as basic as your clothes, haircut or make-up, how are you ever going to let rip in the rest of your life? So remember: when it comes to naughty-but-nice style:

1. BE A DIVA

Also known as love yourself, and love your imperfections. Think of all the famous divas you know; not one of them is apologising for her 'flaws' because one woman's large behind is another's selling point. One woman's extra pounds are a diva's unique sexiness. Being a diva means choosing to feel whatever you want to feel, and acting out that feeling without worrying that you're too old to be stylish, or sexy, or have an attitude. Being a diva also means loving yourself now as opposed to in ten years' time when you'll look back at photos and think, 'Why did I think I was fat/ugly/stupid-looking then?' You can't live for the future and imagine who or what you're going to be when you're thinner, and richer, or married or single. You need to live your life the way you want to now, whatever your circumstances, which means: like a true diva, doing whatever it takes.

2. ESCAPE FROM YOUR EXPECTATIONS

There is a point in many of our lives where we wake up one day and feel trapped. Trapped by our look, trapped by what others think of us and even trapped by our own expectations of what life should be. Take one friend, Susan, 30: she is gorgeous, successful and unhappy. Not just a little unhappy but very unhappy because, despite her glamorous job (she does PR for a very famous band) and her huge income, and that she can have and do whatever she wants, she's not married. As a result, every day she wakes up and feels trapped by her life: 'What if I hadn't gone into PR, I'd have probably met someone by now', or 'What if I didn't have to spend four months a year travelling the world, I'd have more time to boyfriend hunt' are her most popular refrains, despite the fact she gets to see the most amazing places, travel first class and loves her job!

Susan could do with (1) re-evaluating her expectations about what would make her happy; and (2) being a little grateful for what she does already have, because then she would be aware of how every day she is setting herself up for failure. The fact is, like your personal style, you need to re-evaluate your lifestyle on a regular basis, alongside everything else, to see if your expectations still match up to what you want or if they are simply trapping you and governing your life for no reason at all. You can be free of whatever you're disappointed by, by simply looking at your life from a fresh and clean perspective.

3. ACKNOWLEDGE HOW FAR YOU'VE COME

Whenever you feel style-challenged, it can pay to acknowledge how far you've come. I always find photos a very good reminder source for this (and also good for a laugh), so no matter how bad you feel take a look at how you used to look – then remind yourself of all the ways you've changed and are still changing. I say still changing, because when it comes to your style (and your dreams, attitude and sexiness for that matter) a naughty-but-nice take on life is about being in constant motion. Even if you find your perfect look, this isn't something you should still be wearing in five years' time, but a base from which to jump to new looks and new styles so that you never feel stuck again. Just trust in yourself and your decisions, and your naughty style will emerge with less pain than you imagine.

One-month Style Planner

The aim of this month's planner is to bring some style into your life –
think reinvention, restyling and new and more daring looks. This means
de-cluttering your wardrobe, and looking at how you think about your
style and look.

WEEK ONE

Monday   Look at yourself in the mirror and take 10 minutes to consider what your style says about you? Is it hiding your true personality or is it reaching back to a time when you were at your happiest? Are you all in one colour or a victim of fashion?

Tuesday   Think of three things you'd most like to change about your current style? It can be your clothes, your hair, the colours you wear or even how you wear your clothes. Now think of three reasons why you're stuck in a style rut.

Wednesday   Tonight grab a bundle of magazines, flick through them and pull out all the images that portray a style you like. Work out how you can adapt that style to your life. Put the images into a notebook – this is your style and ideas journal.

Thursday   Have a brainstorm with a group of friends you trust and hear what they have to say about your style and what could be improved or changed. Then work out what elements you feel inspired by, what you're going to disregard and what new things you're going to try.

Friday   Prepare for a de-cluttering weekend. Arm yourself with a friend who's an expert in this field as well as bin bags, labels and a vision of who you're aiming to be.

Saturday   De-clutter your wardrobe. Throw out anything you haven't worn in the last year, that doesn't fit, is the wrong colour or that you have never worn. This includes, shoes, bags, jackets, underwear and gifts.

Sunday   Take all your bags to a charity shop and then open up your wardrobe and assess what's left. Think of three new things that are part of the new you and that you now want to buy and put in your wardrobe.

WEEK TWO

Monday   Avoid shopping until you're sure of what you want your new style to say about you and you're able to shop selectively. If you feel the urge focus instead on filling your style journal with images, pictures, and samples of how you see your new style. This is not just about clothes, but make up, interiors and accessories.

Tuesday   Focus on your body image today because how you feel about your body directly corresponds to how you look after yourself and what you choose to wear. Your aim is to see yourself as a 'whole' not as a few good bits and lots of bad parts.

Wednesday   Think about what you could do to improve your body image both internally and externally. Start by thinking about the way you speak to yourself and how you portray yourself to others. Then think about the more practical ways you could improve your body image.

Thursday   Take a long hard look at your shape. It's vital to be able to appraise your shape in a positive way so you can accentuate what you have, as well as disguise and flatter other parts. If you can't do it alone, ask a friend whose style you admire to help restyle you.

Friday   To diminish your self-loathing and judgments about yourself you need to silence the critic within. This is the voice that constantly tells you you're not good enough. Nix it by answering back every time it tries to discourage you. Focus on the fact that the voice is sabotage from within and not the voice of realism.

Saturday   Go into a shop and try on two things you like but you'd never usually wear. Note how they make you feel and in what ways they make you feel good/sexy/different about yourself.

Sunday   Have some fun with your style. Fretting for hours about your look in front of a mirror and fighting back the tears in changing rooms is not the way to find your style. Experimenting and having fun with clothes, hair and make-up is how you'll find your true style and feel happy about it.

WEEK THREE

Monday   Don't be a follower of fashion. Style is supposed to be something that you find enjoyable and inspiring, so don't follow fashion blindly or take the advice of friends who try to turn you into a mini version of them. True style is authentic, so focus on what's in your style journal and how YOU want to look.

Tuesday   Seek help from experts whether it's from magazines or in person. Don't be afraid to ask for help from people in the know. Often they'll know more about what could possibly suit you than you do because they're immersed in the subject and spend all day evaluating other people's styles.

Wednesday   Once you have a clear picture of your new style go shopping. Shop everywhere and try on clothes you'd usually avoid – you don't have to buy them but you'll never know who you could be if you don't try on different looks.

Thursday   If fear is stopping you from changing, take a deep breath and throw away one item from your comfy clothes collection. This will take away your safety net and force you to re-style yourself.

Friday   Spend 30 minutes today thinking outside the box. Take a long, hard look at people in your life. Whose style do you most admire and why? Which famous people do you find yourself searching for in magazines and what is it about their look that you like and admire?

Saturday	Steal other people's style tips, whether it's an amazing beauty product, the way they accessorise or a certain way they do their hair – try it and see if it suits you.
Sunday	Don't let people put you in a box. The moment you start to reinvent yourself all kinds of people will try to put you off, partly because they find change threatening. Stand your ground and do what you have to do for yourself and no one else.

WEEK FOUR

Monday	Think about colour. Colour can lift your mood, change how others respond to you and make you feel confident. To find your best shades look for a colour that complements your hair, skin tone and eyes. The best way to do this is to stand in front of a mirror in good light and place different items of clothing with different colours around your neckline and see what literally lightens up your look.
Tuesday	Think grooming – style is not just about clothes, it's about how you look after yourself. Pampering yourself and focusing on beauty is not shallow, it's simply a sign you care enough about yourself to look after your looks now and again.
Wednesday	Go back to your style journal and note down how far you've come since the beginning of this month and ask yourself – am I closer to who I want to be? What's my new look saying about me? What else would I like to restyle in my life? Remember we're talking reinvention not just fashion.
Thursday	Restyle the rest of your life. Combine all four elements of this book and think about what it would take to restyle your attitude, your vision of your future and the inner you and outer you. Make a list of ten things you'd like to achieve in the next six months.

Friday   Experiment all weekend. Meaning, not only venture out with a new style, but practise acting differently, making different choices and see where it takes you.

Saturday   Flick through an old photo album to remind you how far you've come from who you used to be. Let go of the past and focus on who you are now, but being present and future orientated.

Sunday   Be happy all day! It's a decision, not something that's out of your control. Walk out the door in a look you love, with an attitude that kicks and screams sexy and be focused on going after what you want and need all day.

Conclusion

Style, attitude, your desires, sexiness, and all the naughty aspects we've discussed in this book, are a state of mind. So, like dissatisfaction and disappointment, you can control them. It takes hard work, a brutal and honest look at who you are, and a battle against lifelong behaviours, but hopefully, by now, you've learned you can do it.

I know anyone can undertake a self-esteem makeover and become a happier person because I've seen women transformed (myself included) from big sopping doormats with no self-esteem, to funny, stylish women with guts to go after what they want. And if you think that sounds a little immodest, here's my final point: to live a naughty life you have to be able to acknowledge your accomplishments and say out loud what you're most proud of and what you have achieved.

It's not big-headed to have self-esteem that makes you proud of yourself, and it's not egotistic to feel good about what you've done in your life, and it's certainly not narcissistic to acknowledge that you've come far. Whereas, it is fake and a road to eventual resentment to play down your achievements, because you feel too embarrassed to tell anyone and then feel bitter that no one notices you. And it is a road to sourness to feel jealous because other people are doing what you essentially don't have the balls to do and are willing to stand up and be proud of it. Be yourself – don't succumb to false modesty, and put your efforts into real living instead.

Of course, I can't promise you that leading a naughty-but-nice life will make you richer than anyone else or more perfect or even more successful in a career way, but I do promise you it will make you happier, more content and leave you feeling more like yourself than you have done in years. Why? Well, because naughty living is about being honest with yourself, embracing change rather than running from it, picking yourself up and trying again when you fail, and simply not taking things so seriously, whether you're deciding what it is you want to do with your life, or what it is you are going to wear today!

It's all about freedom, enjoyment and feeling good about who you are every single day without fail. What's more, it's within your grasp right now – so what are you waiting for?

Index